ACROSS THE WINE DARK SEA

DANIEL BRENTS

ISBN: 979-8-90252-115-0   (Paperback)
ISBN: 979-8-90252-116-7   (Hardcover)
ISBN: 979-8-90252-114-3   (eBook)

Printed in the United States of America

CONTENTS

Sailing across the wine dark sea to men of strange speech…

—*The Odyssey*, Homer

FOREWORD

First Adventure

Let's see—the front door is unlocked, and there are no adults around to stop me. I put on my jacket and slip outside. It's a clear, cool day, and the sun is shining in my Detroit neighborhood. Earlier, riding in my dad's car, I saw some interesting things, but we passed them too quickly for me to study. Now I begin my journey, climbing slowly down the steps. At three years old, it feels like a big job. Once I'm steady on the front walk, I know which way I'll go after turning north on the sidewalk. I pass other homes. They're big like mine, but each one is different. I don't know why I know it's north—I just do.

There's a chugging noise up ahead. I wonder what it is. As I draw closer, I see a huge yellow machine with a big motor, making angry rising and falling growling noises as it moves around in a hole it is digging in the earth. Could that be for a basement like mine? I wonder where the coal room and chute will be. That is a really big hole, and the digger shows no sign of stopping. Orange tree roots stick out from the walls it has carved.

After watching for a while, I continue further along the street. Some houses have little flags in their windows—white, with a red border all around and a blue star in the middle. I wonder why we don't have one too. Soon, I come to an empty lot turned into a garden, with wooden stakes, plants and rows of vegetables. I see our neighbor from across the street working there and wonder why he's there instead of in his own yard. I waved, and he waves back and asks me where I'm going. I tell him I'm exploring and then walk on further.

I see a sick bird on the sidewalk, struggling to move. My mom once told me that sick birds can carry germs called diseases, so I don't touch it. I just watch, hoping it will get better and fly. Suddenly a car zooms up, its tires screeching and horn blaring. I turn and see that it's my mom. I can't figure out why she's here. She jumps out of the car, runs toward me, and starts hitting me on my behind with her hand. Almost screaming, she says, "Danny, what do you think you're doing out here?"

I'm confused. Why is she so angry? Why did she spank me? What did I do that was so wrong? Still mad, she grabs me and pushes me into the car. I can't understand why exploring was wrong, but I decide it was worth the spanking anyway.

CHAPTER 1

Youthful Odyssey

I entered college in 1957 as a freshman in architecture in south Texas. In 1958, two of my Dallas boyhood friends—neither of them architecture students—who had joined me in college ran into difficulties and dropped out after our freshman year. Instead, they traveled to Europe through Athens on a Greek freighter, the cheapest way to get there, even less expensive than Icelandic Airlines through Reykjavik. We kept in touch with letters and postcards; there was no email yet. Their messages spoke of strange and curious things, of new wonders and adventures. Locked into my personal trajectory, I longed for similar freedom and adventures.

Some of the other architecture students shared my wanderlust. One spring break, several of us went to Galveston. While there, a few of us came up with the idea of visiting the architectural school at Oklahoma University in Norman. We jumped in a friend's car, sped 360 miles north, and arrived late in the afternoon. The university was also on spring break, but we found one student in the design lab (there was always at least one in an architecture lab) who suggested we might visit the Bavinger House, an experimental design. Its exterior wall was a long, curved spiral made from local sandstone with random chunks of glass set into it to admit light. The structure was anchored by a recycled oil field drill stem that served as a tall central tent pole. It had no interior walls; instead, there were a series of pod-like platforms at different heights, some with curtains that could be drawn for privacy. The ground floor was covered with pools and planted areas. It was both inspiring and informative.

Later, with other aspiring colleagues, we made several spontaneous "field trips" that added to our growing appreciation for the value of unplanned excursions.

Upon graduating, my military draft status became 1A, meaning that if a war broke out, I was a prime candidate to be a grunt in the army at a perilous time of world upheaval—not the kind of adventure I had been hoping for. It would be risky to pursue my dream of traveling, and I had no means of affording it. After some thought, I entered the U.S. Navy Officer Candidate School in Newport, Rhode Island, expecting to "join the Navy and see the world." Shortly afterward, my decision seemed justified by the Cuban Missile Crisis.

With the travel hook firmly set in my mind, I counted the days until I was sworn in as an ensign. In 1963, I was sent to Great Lakes Naval Training Center, north of Chicago, for training. In its recruiting ads, the Navy offered visions of exciting tours of duty in the Mediterranean or the Pacific. My current duties were unclear but kept me busy. One important aspect of training was attending a soirée hosted by the captain in charge of Public Works, the ranking officer in my branch of the Navy Civil Engineer Corps. Other branches included the Seabees and other construction services, which I felt were more appropriate than Public Works, with its emphasis on infrastructure, given my background in architecture.

Following military protocol, I left my calling card in my hat in the vestibule. When the captain's wife introduced herself and inquired about my background, she exclaimed, "Oh, how wonderful! You can help me with the set design for my production of *The Teahouse of the August Moon*!"

Taken aback, I replied, "I'm sorry, ma'am, they're keeping me very busy with my training duties, and I don't know if I'll have the time."

After a stony silence, she replied, "Well, Ensign Brents, we'll have to see that you'll have plenty of time in your permanent assignment." And that's how I got transferred to Fargo, North Dakota.

That's also where I met and married my wife for life, Betty. She came from a small farming community just across the state line in Minnesota and graduated in speech pathology from North Dakota State University. Bright, funny, and caring, she and I had vastly different backgrounds but shared similar values. Most important was the fact that, although she had limited experience of traveling, she was open to adventure.

We moved into a basement apartment in Fargo that was—to put it kindly—spartan. Our space was separated by a hanging rug from the larger part of the basement, which the landlord used as a laundry area. We set up a pair of double bed mattress springs as a divider between the sleeping area and eating area. There was a deep, circular drain hole near the shower (there was no bathroom) that required careful attention from anyone using it.

Privacy was precarious, and when my mother visited, she burst into tears. Still, the rent was only $45 (about $460 today). With my housing and dependents' allowances, I was making close to $2,500 a year (roughly $25,000 today). By watching every penny, we saved aggressively. One evening, when Betty's brother visited, we broke open our piggy bank to scrape together a couple of dollars to take him out in nearby Dilworth, Minnesota. There wasn't that much to do in Dilworth, but that's just what an officer and a gentleman my age did in those days.

It was during this time that we heard the devastating news that President Kennedy had been shot in Dallas, my hometown, at 12:30 p.m. on Friday, November 22, 1963. It was incomprehensible and was soon followed by the announcement of his death. No one knew if the nation—or anyone in it—was safe, or whether it was an opening move by the USSR.

That day, we had been preparing for a trip to Bismark, North Dakota, to attend the wedding of Betty's college classmate. We drove to the wedding, straining to catch each announcement on the radio. I couldn't imagine a worse time for such an event. All of us were glued to the radio and television as more details emerged. The wedding reception was a sad, brief affair. To many of us, it seemed the beginning of an endless national nightmare—soon after followed by the deaths of Martin Luther King and Robert Kennedy, and then by the debacle of the war in Vietnam.

My first assignment in Fargo involved the challenging responsibility of supervising the patching of a damaged asphalt area in the Navy recruiting station's parking lot. Soon after, I was appointed resident officer in charge of construction for the development of a training missile storage facility for the Air National Guard, adjacent to Fargo's airport, Hector Field. It was a useful experience, although somewhat less than exciting, as the duties resembled those in the construction administration phase of the architectural world, in which the work is monitored to ensure compliance with contract documents—drawings and specifications. I was given the use of a Navy pickup truck, equipped with a shovel in its bed. If I got stuck in the plentiful North Dakota mud, I could use it to shovel sand from the back of the truck.

Some, including me, might wonder what the Navy was doing in North Dakota. I was told that when the Air Force was formed as a separate branch of the military from the Army, Congress required it, as a precondition, to farm out all its construction work to either the Army or the Navy. It was about as far from my expectations as possible when I joined the Navy OCS.

Evidently, my performance was sufficiently acceptable that I was granted oversight of a second Air National Guard training missile facility, this time in Des Moines, Iowa. As in Fargo, I reported to civil service managers—one assigned to accompany me and keep me from making mistakes and another back in Great Lakes to monitor both of us. Practice makes perfect! I was promoted to lieutenant junior grade, and my pay was upgraded accordingly, to about $38,000 in today's money.

Still saving aggressively, in Des Moines we upgraded our housing to an apartment above a laundromat, located at the noisy intersection of two of the city's primary truck routes, with a convenient entrance directly off the laundromat's parking lot. Hot water came from an ancient heater in the kitchen, with a pop-off valve that offered unpredictable bursts of steam.

From time to time, we drove back to Minnesota to see Betty's family, occasionally braving blinding snowstorms and dodging tornados. A local radio station in Mankato, Iowa, once asked listeners to be on the lookout for Farmer Hawkins' henhouse. During many of these visits, we would drop in on some of Betty's friends. Whenever we mentioned our plans to travel to Europe, the usual response was "Why would you want to do that?" To them, it seemed impractical, expensive, and risky. They were wrong about the expensive part; we had managed to scrape together $3,000, or about $30,000 in today's dollars. On top of that, we had scoured Arthur Frommer's 1957 book *Europe on 5 Dollars a Day*. That works out to be $1,825 a year, leaving us about $2,175 to get there and back. Totally doable! And "impractical" and "risky" sounded just right to us.

In 1965, I was discharged from the Navy. We went back to Dallas, where I found work as an architectural draftsman. I had no intention of remaining there; I was simply waiting for my Europe travel plan to materialize, which it did within only six weeks.

I had stayed in touch with my friends who had dropped out of college. One of them, Brad, had returned from Europe to New York and worked as a stone sculptor under the tutelage of Alfred Van Loen, a noted German modernist. Brad's aunt was deeply involved in Manhattan theater, and he assimilated easily. I visited him and his wife, Verna, during my Navy years, in their fourth-floor walk-up, rent-controlled apartment in Greenwich Village, where he gave me lots of travel advice. My long-range plan was to join him in New York and take up painting instead of architecture. Brad offered us the storage space in his basement for our belongings during our journey to Europe, and I was glad to accept. At the time, Greece was an attractive destination because of its history, cultural heritage, and affordability. Italy and Spain also appealed, although less strongly. This was when those countries were still less developed and before the French discovered toll roads, which ultimately rendered it to be decidedly not cheap.

While in New York, Brad and Verna invited me to join them at a Vietnam protest rally. I was unhappy with our government's intervention in Vietnam, so I agreed to go. The anti-war movement was gathering momentum. The rally, held in a Midtown theater auditorium, began with angry speeches. I agreed with most of it, until the speakers and audience began to berate the young people they accused of enabling the war by serving in combat. That was too much for me, and I stood up and left. From that point on, I remained terribly conflicted. I admired the young men who endured combat but despised the government officials responsible for sending them to risk or give their lives. In my view, Kennedy, Johnson, McNamara, Rusk, Dulles, Kissinger, Bundy, Westmoreland, and their supporters were guilty of unjustified manslaughter simply to remain in power; the young men were largely guiltless. I remained conflicted for years. It was a time of worldwide generational upheaval and effectively created civil divisions that still affect us in the U.S. today.

Following Brad's suggestion, in 1965, I booked passage for Betty and me to Athens on a Greek freighter from Hellenic Lines. I quit my job in Dallas after only six weeks, and we left for New York. While we waited for the ship to arrive, we stayed with Brad and Verna. One afternoon Brad suggested going out for lunch, saying, "How do you like Afghan food?" We had never even thought of it, but this was another kind of experience we had never encountered before. It was strange but fun. Brad had to return to his studio afterward, so we set out to sightsee. While walking, a woman came toward us with a small lapdog on a leash. The dog skipped toward Betty, circled her feet, and barked until she tripped to the sidewalk. The dog's owner, in a thick Manhattan accent, exclaimed, "Laiydee, watch out for the *duwaog*!" The woman went on her way, concerned only for her mutt. I helped Betty back up, and we both felt we had learned something about the nation's biggest city.

CHAPTER 2

Anchors Aweigh

It was March when at last, our ship came in. Late one afternoon, we went to the wharf in Brooklyn, boarded, and found our cabin. After about an hour, we were asked to come to the wardroom—the dining room—to meet the captain and the other passengers. The captain was known simply as "Captain." Crew members included Mitsos, or Dimitrios, who served in the mess, and Stephanos, who was assigned to keep tabs on us passengers. Among the travelers was an ancient fellow of about sixty years of age named Yannis, returning to Greece after visiting his son in the Midwest, and two illegals, Giorgos and Eirini. Giorgos had evaded extradition from the U.S. by overstaying his visa, and Eirini was a Greek student and Vietnam protester who had irritated the Johnson administration with her noisy, outspoken views. The administration had lost patience with young, irresponsible whippersnappers and Commie sympathizers, whose children and grandchildren are often viewed the same way today. As it turned out, Eirini had gone to college with one of Betty's girlhood friends in Minnesota. Sharing her opinion of the war in Vietnam, we spent time with her while on board.

The departure was a completely exhilarating moment, and we felt a great sense of relief and excitement—freedom from everything of the past. I had read actor Sterling Hayden's book *Wanderer*, in which he described his reckless adventure at sea in his sailboat. For us, there would be no more imposed routines, no obligations. In a fit of excitement, I tore off my Timex watch and threw it into the ocean to celebrate my final discharge from my past—my parents, my career trajectory, my military service, all of it. It was a thrilling moment to pass under the

Verrazano Bridge before sunset and out into the open sea. In that instant, our future seemed to expand like fireworks in the sky.

Everyone on board felt sorry for our ignorance of the Greek language, and over the course of our month or more at sea, we learned the basics—hello, goodbye, good morning, and so on. I've always felt that French is the most beautiful of languages, while Greek, to my ear, seems guttural. I suspect the Greek language was influenced by Turkish during the centuries of Ottoman occupation. The word for "sea" in the lyrical French language is a blunt *mer,* but one the most beautiful words in the Greek language, perhaps of any language, is *thalassa* for sea. One can almost feel the waves lapping at the shore in that beautiful word. It makes me think of Homer's tales.

Long days and nights slipped by, including one that was truly dark and stormy. Under dark, soaking skies, the waves tossed the toy-like ship and its passengers like bobbing corks or drunken sailors, and the bow periodically sank beneath angry waves. I now realized why the tables and other flat surfaces in the ship's dining room were surrounded by a metal rim raised about a quarter inch above the surface: to keep the tableware from crashing to the floor.

We ate our meals with the others in the dining room, carefully picking through a wholly new cuisine. Among my favorites were *dolmadas*—grape leaves stuffed with rice, meat and spices; *moussaka,* a layered dish of spiced meat, eggplant, and potatoes; and *pastitsio,* featuring feta, minced beef, crushed tomato, and pasta. Yannis, the old gentleman, showed us how to drink Greek coffee, served in a *demi-tasse* like expresso, with half a cup full of grounds. Legend had it that when the cup was turned over onto the saucer after drinking, the grounds would foretell the future with their Rorschach-like pattern. For Easter, the cook prepared a traditional soup known as *magaritsa*—a bowl of spicy vegetables floating in a fragrant broth with half a lamb's head, brain-side up. There was general hilarity as we excused ourselves from the table.

We learned that Greece was undergoing a similar malaise to that in the U.S.—a giant political struggle pitting the then-current democratic government, led by Konstantin Karamanlis, against a junta of rebellious colonels under Giorgos Papadopoulos. Youth were solidly against the threat of repression and angrily resisted the junta, though the colonels tightened their grip on power through brute force, aided by the apathy and acquiescence of the conservative citizenry at large. Although the coup did not affect us directly, it seeped around the edges of daily life. It made us fearful for our own democracy, given the instability of the times.

The long days were followed by empty nights, and the captain prepared entertainment for passengers and crew. He announced a movie night, had the crew set up a projector and screen, and we took our seats in the dining room, expecting perhaps an informative travelogue or a dramatic film about Greek life, such as *Never on Sunday*. What we watched instead was a film called *Digging for Gold*. It opened with a statuesque young blonde woman in a rocky landscape, clad in a man's white shirt, carrying a pickaxe. She attacked nearby stones, but the work was evidently hot, and she repeatedly wiped her brow. At last, exasperated, she slowly removed her shirt—unfortunately having forgotten her bra. Refreshed, she enthusiastically resumed her quest for riches, at which point Betty and I looked at each other with puzzlement.

More days slowly passed, and again the captain made another attempt to relieve our boredom. This time he announced a "Scotch Night," with drinks for the passengers "on the house," so to speak. For some while, he had been eyeing the young female passenger, Eirini, who was our age, and half his. He carefully managed to keep her glass constantly topped off, but unfortunately for him, she paid more attention to Giorgos, who was nearer her age. The night wore on, and all of us were reluctant to turn in, though eventually the two of us did so.

Sound asleep, we were jolted awake early in the morning by a blast from the ship's foghorn. Fearing we had struck an iceberg, we scrambled out to the deck, where the disheveled captain was supervising a haphazard lifeboat and safety-vest drill with his bullhorn. It was curious timing, coming well into our voyage.

When the captain noticed us, he announced over his bullhorn, "I'm sorry, Mrs. Brents, but this is necessary." Yet when he saw that Eirini and Giorgos had not appeared, he put two and two together, perhaps they were in Giorgos' cabin. He became very upset that his efforts had failed and began yelling through his bullhorn, "Eirini, Eirini, where are you?" After several unrewarding repetitions, the bullhorn shut off with an electronic squawk, and he called off the drill.

Later that morning, as we approached the port in Tripoli, Libya, scores of dolphins glided and leapt through the green water beside the ship, as though playfully escorting us to shore. We docked, and from the hold rose hundreds of cases of Budweiser beer in nets, bound for the U.S. Wheelus Air Force Base near the kingdom's capital. The ship would remain in harbor for several hours before sailing on to Greece, so Betty and I chose to wander in an Arab Muslim country for the first time. Meanwhile, the captain selflessly offered the crew and other male passengers an opportunity to visit a local brothel, the location of which he somehow happened to know.

It was our first chance to see women swathed from head to toe in their black robes, or *abayas,* and our first glimpse of mosques. The gasoline stations were all branded AGIP, an entity owned by the Italian energy company Eni, whose logo was a six-legged, fire-breathing dog. We had never before visited a casino, and upon learning there was one nearby, we asked for directions. It was another adventure, like going to Rick's Bar in *Casablanca.* After wandering through the tables, I eventually decided to take a wild chance and buy a five-dollar chip. I had never played roulette before, but I tentatively placed the bet on black. The wheel spun with a loud clacking noise, and I turned away, certain that I had wasted our money. Then behind me, I heard the *tap, tap, tap* of the croupier's stick on my chip. I thought I had surely done something wrong. I returned to the table, and the croupier pushed a stack of chips toward me then motioned for me to bet again or leave.

When I cashed the chips in, I was paid in Libyan pounds issued by King Idris. These were of a curious design, featuring a human iris centered above a royal shield. I thereafter thought of Libya's king as King Iris. When I took the notes to another teller, I found I had made eighty dollars on my five-dollar bet. It was an auspicious beginning, and we were happy with the diversion.

After weighing anchor, we soon landed at Piraeus, the port of Athens. As an architectural student, I studied specific sites there, but I knew nothing of the contemporary city, which was bustling and chaotic. There seemed little reason or thought to the organization of streets, which doubtless followed well-worn pathways from long ago, nor purpose in the placement of things. It all felt haphazard but exciting. We found an affordable hotel, dropped off our backpacks, and hit the streets. Making way along the busy thoroughfares, we immediately encountered our first major problem: street signs, warning signs, directional signs—all written not just in a different language, but also with a different alphabet, which we later learned was derived from ancient Phoenician. Tourism was new in Greece, and only a few people spoke English. Somehow, we made it to Syntagma Square, in the center of Athens, where we watched Greek soldiers in costumes march while changing the guard at the tomb of their unknown soldier.

For the remainder of the day, we wandered through the streets, absorbing the very different way of life, with numerous outdoor conversations and salesmen's calls—all unintelligible. A common conveyance was a donkey pulling a cart, moving goods around instead of a motor vehicle. Some donkeys had their manes dyed orange, perhaps to make it easier for their owners to find them.

One morning, while we were out, Betty wore a pair of pink denims. She was greeted with numerous catcalls of "Hello, sir" and "Hello, mister" because Greek men had never seen a woman wearing pants in the sixties.

Of course, we made our way to the acropolis, where we saw the Propylaea, the Doric ceremonial entrance, and the Erectheion, with its beautiful Caryatids—columns in the forms of women, carved from marble, holding up the roof of the porch. Just beyond stood the Parthenon, the former temple of Athena, built in the fifth century BCE to celebrate victory over Persian invaders. It was later used as an ammunition dump by the Ottomans and struck by a Venetian bomb in the 1600s. The site remains in ruins as a result, and one must use imagination to appreciate the beauty of the complex as it once was. I was fascinated by the scale of it—the balance of ingenuity, design, craftsmanship, and determination required to erect it, and the evidence of these qualities in the civilization that achieved it. It made me think of the treasures they left us: art, philosophy, mathematics, myths, drama, and more. These people had their problems, but they were incredibly modern and inquisitive. I felt a deep kinship from across the centuries, not for the last time.

In the afternoons and evenings, we wandered through the Plaka, an old village area just below the acropolis, full of tinsmiths, salesmen hawking goat hair rugs, cramped little cafés, and other tourist bait. At night, we ate *souvlaki*, delicious lamb or chicken roasted on skewers, and drank *retsina*, Greece's annoying resinated version of wine. We listened to musicians playing their *bouzoukis* and watched men dance the celebratory *sirtaki* or other complicated forms of dance that vary by region or celebratory event.

One evening, we met an elderly Spanish fellow whose English was quite good. We enjoyed his company and toasted with *ouzo*, a very powerful anise or licorice-flavored alcoholic beverage usually cut by half with water. As we sat, we talked about poetry and many other things.

To me, poetry is closely tied to music and abstract painting— forms that express what cannot otherwise be said yet move us both emotionally and intellectually. One might write or say, "The trees were whispering to my companion, but I could not hear" or consider the thought-provoking abstract works of painters such as Gerhardt Richter.

I knew next to nothing about poetry but remembered an article I had recently read about the Spanish poet Federico Lorca. Our new friend picked up on this with great excitement, asked Betty to dance, and ordered more ouzo. Something about the encounter seemed unusual, but later I learned that I had unintentionally opened a new topic. Lorca, the poet I had pretended to have read, was gay, and evidently so was our newfound friend. We nonetheless enjoyed him and were grateful for his company.

One morning, we received a message at our hotel from the ship's captain, inviting us to join him for dinner in Piraeus. We were puzzled but not inclined to refuse a free meal. We gladly accepted and made our way to the seaside restaurant. Though crowded, the captain ordered for just the three of us. Soon a giant lobster, easily eighteen inches long, appeared, together with some black, round, spiny creatures we learned were sea urchins. To eat them, one had to crack the shells open, squeeze lemon juice on them to kill them, and then swallow them like oysters. We made an effort but then settled for the lobster, which at least was recognizable. The captain did not explain why we were singled out for such a favor, but we later concluded that it was an attempt to dissuade us from reporting his shipboard behavior to his employer, Hellenic Lines.

I was a big fan of the author Nikos Kazantzakis, who was from the Greek island of Crete. Kazantzakis wrote *Zorba the Greek*, a portrait of a larger-than-life-figure—energetic, insightful, brimming with homespun wisdom—a perfect hero for an adventurous young man such as I imagined myself.

Crete is an island off the south of Greece and was accessible by an overnight ferry from Piraeus to Heraklion, its major city. Nearby is Knossos, the center of the ancient Minoan civilization. I believe the ferry carried roughly two hundred people who perished when it sank a few years after our journey. On that overnight trip, passengers were divided by gender. Many removed their shoes before climbing into their bunks, and before long the stench was overpowering. Returning to the outside deck, I searched for a water fountain. Instead, I found a large glass jug of water with a string tied to its neck at one end and a metal cup at the other. This was ancient Greek hygiene. Betty soon joined me on deck, and together we waited for sunrise.

Landing at Heraklion, we set out to find a youth hostel. Along the way, the delicious smell of fresh-baked bread followed us at every turn. We hurried past stalls of fly-covered hanging goat and lamb carcasses and stopped at a bakery for a round loaf of baked bread, honey, and coffee. We planned to stay overnight, eager to reach nearby Knossos. Knossos was the site of the myths involving Theseus, Ariadne, Daedalus and Icarus, and the Minotaur. It was partially restored by British archeologist Sir Arthur Evans, whose renovations have since been judged inaccurate. Nevertheless, it was inspiring to see the frescoes, the snake goddess figurines, the wall decorations of ocean waves, bull jumpers, and the bull-horn sculpture. We saw the *megaron*, the great multipurpose hall, at the heart of the palace, the granary with its immense clay storage vessels, and the impressive drainage system. We did not see the mythical labyrinth, but the entire palace itself seemed to resemble one. We knew much of what we saw was a distorted reconstruction, yet it was thrilling to walk through a site first established nearly four thousand years earlier, rebuilt several times after fire and earthquake. It was something we could never experience back home.

Filled with curiosity, we decided to continue south to Phaistos, on the island's southern coast. Phaistos was the second largest Minoan palace in Crete, about an hour away by car, but we caught a ride from a southbound truck who took us part way. It was a beautiful day, and we decided to walk a while through fields and meadows, over hills and valleys. It was so peaceful. For an hour, we hadn't seen a soul, until, crossing another field, we noticed a figure striding toward us. Nervous, we thought that the owner might chase us away.

As he approached, I said "Good morning" in Greek. He was a striking, formidable-looking man in traditional Cretan costume: dressed in black, with a beret, a red sash at his waist, and black leather jackboots reaching to his knees. He was Zorba the Greek personified.

Frowning, he asked something that I couldn't understand, so I repeated, "Good morning" in English. He looked stunned for a moment, then exclaimed, "Jesus Christ, Americans!"

He asked us to come with him to his nearby cottage, explaining that he had once been a taxi driver in Chicago. Delighted to encounter us, he described the Greek tradition of welcoming unknown strangers, rooted in the ancient belief that the gods sometimes appeared as mortals on doorsteps. He made us coffee and admitted that he had worried we were "tomato-eaters"—the local name for German youths who camped in the open fields and ate the farmers' tomatoes. He also told us that many Greeks had an unfounded belief that money grows on trees in America.

We left him with gratitude for his warm welcome and continued south. At dusk we reached the shore, where a tiny tavern stood at the edge of a stunning Mediterranean beach. The tavern owner greeted us and explained that this was the ancient port of Phaistos, and we had missed palace site itself. Weary, hungry, short on daylight, and feeling the first effects of bronchitis, we gladly accepted his invitation to share a meal and a night's rest in his guest quarters. The meal was a simple omelet, and the quarters were cold and damp, but we were in no position to haggle.

The next morning we awoke to a view of the seaside beach and sparkling azure waters, with a limestone cliff rising nearby in which there were several caves. The place was called Matala. When we asked our host about the caves, he said they were ancient, abandoned funerary sites, now used as bedrooms by wandering youths like ourselves. Burning with curiosity, we crossed the sandy beach and immediately encountered some of these troglodytes—British and Australians travelers. Some had only just arrived while others had been there for months. They showed us one unoccupied cave, which we claimed. Another cave was empty, but it was known as the "shit cave."

We exchanged names. One American couple we would later meet again was Stephan and Karen. His uncle had arranged their passage on his ship, and she was from the Midwest. Stephan drove a black BMW motorcycle, and they were traveling and smoking hashish. We had no idea what hash was and no interest in trying it, nor did we smoke weed. We were that rarest of creatures in our age—"straight" hippies. We learned later that Bob Dylan, Joan Baez, and Joni Mitchell "discovered" and visited Matala three years afterward, along with numerous other hippies. Still later, the Greek junta closed the site, condemning it as a disgrace. We had rarely been so avant-garde.

Afterward, we hitchhiked farther across Crete. Leaving Matala, we saw a man driving a Volkswagen, which wasn't unusual. The Beetle's rear engine meant its trunk was in the front. What made this one exceptional was a marble column clamped upright in the front trunk like a big cigar. Evidently, some temple somewhere was missing its column. On the north coast, we met some German kids who invited us to try some artichokes they had bought. We had never eaten them before, so we obligingly chewed and swallowed a leaf. It was not a wonderful treat. It was another learning experience as they showed us how to scrape the meat off the top of the leaf with our teeth.

Later, we were back in the Peloponnese, south of mainland Greece. We found an inexpensive motel south of Mycenae, the onetime home of the legendary Agamemnon. We had dinner and an argument. Today, neither of us can remember what it was about. As a result, Betty refused to visit the ruins the following morning. So I went alone. I wished she had come with me. I saw the Lion Gate, the corbeled beehive tombs, and the tunnel leading down to the underground spring that had enabled the inhabitants to survive sieges. Nearby stood the theater of Epidaurus, magnificently preserved. It was theater in the half-round, with acoustics that were remarkable.

Still in the Peloponnese Peninsula, we visited Olympia, site of the ancient Olympic Games, and temporary truce between competing nation states. The sanctuary had also housed a gigantic ivory-and-gold statue of Zeus, one of the seven wonders of the ancient world. Now it was mostly in ruins. Segments of massive columns splayed across the ground, toppled like stacks of coins pushed over. What I loved best was the ancient stadium, its start and finish lines still clearly marked by buried stones. The distance measured the standard Olympic *Stade*—192 meters, or about 630 feet. I ran the length, although without a watch I couldn't time myself.

Next, back in mainland Greece, we went to Delphi, the cliffside site of Pythia, the oracle of Apollo on Mount Parnassus. She had been famous for delivering cryptic prophecies to those seeking Apollo's guidance on major decisions. The site had been rebuilt several times, including during Roman occupation, and the ruins remain confusing, made more so by the haphazard "treasuries" erected by various city-states to commemorate victories. That night we found refuge in a nearby hostel, where we met a charming motorcyclist from Goa named Jerry. We had never heard of Goa, on the western edge of India, but we enjoyed his company. Leaving Delphi the next day, we caught a ride with a delightful French couple in their Citroën. It was by far the most pleasant and comfortable of our hitchhiking experiences.

As we prepared to leave Greece, we went to the seaside city of Nafplion, where we would board a ferry to Italy. Nafplion lies just five kilometers—about three miles—south of Tiryns, the home of Hercules.

We were tiring of Greece by then, but stopping at a local café in Nafplion, we decided on lunch. As we ate, the owner and a cook came to our table and urged us to try a "special" Greek dish. I shrugged and said why not, and they brought a small plate of what looked like fried dumplings. I took a bite. They were chewy, and I said they didn't taste especially good. They assured me that they would get better the more I ate. Suspicious of their snickering, I looked more closely. I had never had mountain oysters before, but I was reasonably sure that I had done so now. At this, the two men broke into guffaws. Not surprisingly, they didn't get a tip, and we were completely ready to say *"toso kairo"* (so long) to Greece.

The "Sick Man of Europe" is an appellation first used by Czar Nicholas I to describe the Ottoman Empire. In recent times, it has been applied to Greece, Italy, and France. Greece earned the sobriquet after joining the EU in 1981, suffering economic challenges that led to bailout programs and austerity measures, finally regaining its footing in 2022. The problems of the past included an ultraconservative, isolationist population governed for many years by a corrupt and repressive military junta. Although we enjoyed its vivid experiences, including glimpses of civilizations long gone, it was clear that much time would be required for that nation to be on par with the rest of Europe.

We caught a ferry from Nafplion to Naples and a new, unknown language—though this time in a Roman alphabet. Italian was in some respects like Spanish, which I had studied before, but it was easy to get myself in trouble. I don't remember much about this time in Naples, but I do remember that we caught a bus to Pompeii. When we arrived, we bypassed the many guides looking for customers (we were on a tight budget—a stupid choice I regretted often and rectified later), so we took off on our own. We were struck by the narrow streets with their stepping-stone crosswalks with spaces between them for chariot wheels and drainage. It was fascinating to see the damaged frescos, depicting inhabitants, their daily life, beliefs, and pastimes.

Although we saw the remains of the city and the plaster replicas of some of its inhabitants in their death throes, the lack of a guide to help us understand how the puzzle pieces fit together was a serious shortcoming, relieved only by later visits and future excavations. It was shortsightedness born of penny-pinching, which characterized this entire adventure, although it allowed us to gain other insights, and was mediated in the future. The opportunity to visit a nearly two-thousand-year-old urban complex was truly unique and compelling rather than viewing artifacts in a museum or ruins of a palace or a temple devoid of context.

As we left, passing Mount Vesuvius, I couldn't help thinking about the proximity of Naples' current exurbs near the volcano. These people were risking everything on the fact that Vesuvius had slept for centuries. Sure, the soil was rich and the housing cheaper, but they might also become a tourist site in the future. Living there could be risky, as I felt later in my life when I was diagnosed with an aortic aneurysm. Sudden death could come at any random moment.

We quickly visited Rome, where we saw the Colosseum and the Pantheon. On the Via dei Fori Imperiali, we saw maps of the Roman Empire, erected by Mussolini to mobilize and embolden later-day Romans during his reign by reminding them of their historic conquests—though the comparison was hardly flattering. These maps showed Rome's expansion over five centuries. Mussolini's rule lasted only twenty-one years and captured but a fraction of Rome's empire. The only traces of his architectural footprints are a few scattered examples of "Mussolini Modern," designed by architect Marcello Piacentini, the Italian counterpart of Hitler's Albert Speer.

Another place we visited was Florence, but the difference here was the hostel where we stayed. The youth rumor mill—those frequently fallible stories that circulated among fellow vagabonds—postulated that it had once been Mussolini's villa. It was certainly big enough and carried the presence of a fading movie star, so who knows? The kitchen served delicious and memorable spaghetti Bolognese.

Among its remarkable features was a marble staircase, and one evening we saw an American girl walking down it with heavy cords in each hand, tied to her feet. She descended very carefully, in obvious pain. We asked how she got injured, and she explained that she was riding back from Genoa on a Vespa motor scooter she and her boyfriend had bought there. In a tunnel outside of Genoa, a car in front of them suddenly stopped, causing the crash. We sympathized with her and then started thinking. We had gotten tired of depending on hitchhiking and train fares. What if we went to Genoa and bought a Vespa? It seemed like a great idea! We had slept in caves and saved money. We felt bulletproof and promised ourselves we would be extra careful in tunnels, so it made perfect sense. We went to Genoa and bought a Vespa.

In northern Italy we traveled to Venice and then crossed the border into Austria. We visited Vienna with its *Rungstrasse* (Ringroad) and bought a tent and some camping equipment. In Vienna we dropped into a *rathskeller* for a beer. Two Austrian men joined us at our table, and we started a conversation. One of them was on crutches. He began talking about how great Hitler had been, and how the Nazis were cheated out of victory. We didn't finish our beers. Afterward, we passed though the southern tip of Bavaria, where Hitler's *Berchtesgaden* or Eagle's Nest stood, a kind of German Camp David. We didn't stop.

Later, we drove to Salzburg and were surprised to discover that they also observed siesta time. We attended a wonderful chamber music performance in a lovely hall and afterward found duvets on our hotel beds. Duvets always made me uncomfortably warm, and from then on, whenever I encountered one, I would pull out the stuffing and sleep beneath the doubled sheets.

From there, our travels carried us to snow-blanketed mountain roads in Switzerland and across into France, where we enjoyed the warm sunshine, camping sites, and tuna sandwiches with Port Salut cheese and red wine. We drove to the beaches at Arromanches and Normandy, where we saw the wide-open sands with German pillboxes above them. At the U.S. cemetery, we walked among the thousands of stone grave markers, read a moving letter from the local mayor—thankful for the sacrifices of so many young lives—and tried to hold back tears. As we drove near the site, we noticed a few cars from Germany. Doubtless they were headed to the nearby German cemetery to pay respects.

After falling off the Vespa while trying to climb a hill, we took a ferry from Calais to Dover. In England, we camped at the Chrystal Palace campground. Our top priority was to see the Neolithic remains at Avebury and Stonehenge. At the latter, we were free to wander and even climb on fallen monoliths. We also visited the Roman Baths and Oxford, where we returned decades later to join The Oxford Experience, an adult series of courses offered to the general public. There we stayed in Christ Church College and ate in the great hall where *Harry Potter* was filmed. Next, we crossed into Wales and Ireland, where, among other things, we kissed the Blarney Stone.

Crossing back into France, we set out for Perpignan, on the border with Spain. Traveling through Spain, we sold the Vespa to two Spanish men for about half what we had paid for it and continued on to Lisbon, hoping to catch a flight back to New York on TAP, the Portuguese airline. Eventually we made it back to New York, where we waited for a new car—a Volkswagen Squareback—to be shipped from Germany to New Jersey.

During our trip, we had agreed that we probably couldn't survive on sales from my artwork, and that instead of pursuing painting in New York, we would be smarter to move to San Francisco, where I would look for work as an architectural draftsman. And so, we picked up our new car and left for California.

CHAPTER 3

The Interim

When I was a student learning the craft of architecture, no one told us about economic cycles. Returning from Europe, I discovered for myself in San Francisco that they can be dangerous, especially for beginners. The field is particularly sensitive to recessions, and I learned quickly that young, relatively inexperienced practitioners are especially vulnerable. Betty had no such difficulty; with her previous experience as a welfare worker, she quickly found a job with a modest salary in San Francisco. Eventually, I secured work at a firm willing to hire rank beginners like me and pay them an almost living wage. However, I found that it was very tough for us to make ends meet on our combined income, and if we were to have children, it would be impossible. When Betty became pregnant with our first son, Alan, in 1968, it did become impossible.

I had grown dissatisfied with architectural design, which led my contemporaries to treat each building as a standalone sculpture, without regard for its context or surroundings. I changed the direction of my career, pursuing a master's degree in urban design with a focus on master planning. As a veteran, I was eligible for the G.I. Bill of Rights, which covered tuition fees, books, and housing. With Betty working, we could only just survive in graduate school.

I enrolled in a graduate program in architecture and urban design at Washington University in St. Louis. The program lasted only two semesters, but with stronger qualifications, I could improve my job prospects. I completed the program and managed to join an up-and-coming firm in Baltimore known for urban design. We packed our family and belongings into the Squareback and left for Baltimore. Our financial situation became more tenuous, as the new position wasn't much more rewarding and our second son was on the way. Still, the firm's work was far more interesting and challenging, and I thoroughly enjoyed it and the people I worked with. They were being considered for ever more interesting projects.

After a few years, I longed to be closer to my aging parents, and my pay and advancement opportunities had stagnated as the "guns and butter" recession triggered by Vietnam took hold. I eventually found work for a deservedly little-known firm in Dallas, and we moved there in 1972. But the national economy grew much worse in 1973 with the Arab oil embargo. When the economy was flat, the market for real estate went down, and all my options were limited. One promising arena remained: overseas. There was little competition, as many domestic firms with marketable skills viewed the overseas market as too risky or too challenging. Without adequate preparation, they were right to do so.

I had no opportunities for major travel other than family vacations in Mexico with Betty. Eventually, I found work in a firm that had "international" in its name. They were building teams of experienced designers and project managers for work in the Middle East and Asia but were based in the U.S. As a result, they were bringing modern design and technology to new markets where these skills were needed by clients that could easily afford them but had to import them.

CHAPTER 4

Back in the Arena

I no sooner than joined the new firm in Austin in 1966 when I found myself on an airplane bound for Dhahran—the major city in the eastern province of Saudi Arabia—with a stopover in Zurich. The firm was then designing a huge regional royal palace for the king and his retinue, but it had also secured numerous sizeable projects in the kingdom for ARAMCO, the Arab and American oil company based in Dhahran. We managed not only the design but also the procurement of construction materials and furnishings for those projects.

Zurich was great—schnitzel, a sauna, and rest. On a return trip, in that same sauna, some Europeans remarked how foolish America had been to elect that actor, Ronald Reagan, as president.

The following day, our Swiss Air flight took us over the Alps and southward. Later, the pilot announced we would land in Dhahran. Immediately, several young women in bright tops and skintight jeans rose up and headed aft, for the bathrooms. Minutes later they returned, swathed in black robes and veils. The transformation was astonishing. As we descended into the darkness, the landscape below was dotted by orange flames. I later learned that these were methane gas flares, exhausted as a waste product from hundreds of drilling rigs. The sight was somehow disturbing as we arrived in the hellish landscape.

Landing at Dhahran International, we gathered our belongings and disembarked. Although it was evening, the air was still hot—over 95 degrees—and saturated with humidity. We lined up for customs, and my traveling companion warned me what to expect. It was a madhouse.

Orderly queues quickly broke into mobs as tired, stressed Arabs jostled with drunken Europeans and grumpy Yanks. Many Arabs carried huge boxes, televisions, refrigerators, and other items unavailable in the kingdom. The scene was filled with unintelligible yelling, pushing, and stifling heat—there was no air conditioning. I was told that any baggage approved by custom agents (the ones in robes, although of course all the Arabs were in robes) would be marked with a chalk check. I was advised to place my bags against a wall afterward, turning the chalk mark inward so it couldn't be rubbed off. The voice of experience. Novice visitors were outraged when agents confiscated their whiskey, tore out magazine pages featuring liquor ads, uncomplimentary news about the United Arab Republic's recent attack from Egypt on Israel, or women in skimpy costumes. It was the ninth circle of hell.

A young architect from our firm, already stationed there for several weeks, guided me to his Chevy Suburban, the standard Aramco vehicle, and drove me to our company's rental apartment in the city. I was exhausted and could have enjoyed a beer, but not in the kingdom. I collapsed into bed.

Suddenly, I was awakened by loud clanking noises. People were walking through the dark streets banging pots and pans. It was Ramadan, the month for fasting in Islamic countries, and these folks were alerting their neighbors that sunrise was coming, and they would no longer be permitted to eat, drink, or have sex during the daytime.

Checking in for work, I met Bev, a blond, middle-aged American woman in Aramco's HR department, who wore heavy plastic glasses frames. She took my passport and quizzed me about my background. Several flies buzzed around, and Bev told me to get used to them, calling them the Saudi national bird.

Back in the States, the firm had given us new employees a series of indoctrination lessons about Saudi culture. We learned that the two officially acknowledged genders were rigidly separated in school and the workplace, and women's rights were nonexistent. At that time, women were not permitted to drive and must always be accompanied by a male relative in public. The religious police, or *mutawa*, enforced these and other cultural taboos, often beating violators with canes. Ordinary visitors who had traveled in Israel were required to carry those visas and entry-exit stamps on a separate removeable passport page. Alcohol was forbidden for import or sale, although Westerners were permitted to manufacture and consume it privately. In fact, American Aramco employees circulated an underground pamphlet describing how to brew homemade liquor, known as the "Blue Flame." Occasionally, in the Aramco residential compound, there would be an accidental explosion from a faulty still. The concoction was called *sadiqi*, or "little friend." It came in two varieties: brown, supposedly resembling scotch or bourbon, and white, supposedly gin or vodka. Both could be quite potent. More than a few Aramcons were alcoholics out of the lack of healthier pastimes.

This was in the days when many Saudis were still Bedouins and often uneducated. The population was relatively small, and most skilled jobs were filled by immigrants. In Riyadh, the capital city, a Saudia Airlines aircraft that had been taking workers back to Pakistan was left a burned-out hulk sidelined off the runway because a passenger started a fire in its aisle to boil tea. It was not unusual to see locals serving Aramco in menial roles, such as sentries living in tents near the compound, surrounded by trash. In the desert where most had previously lived, trash would either be blown away immediately or covered by sand, and there were no disposal or collection sites. A pickup truck driving in the town with two camels in the back was a frequent sight, and I will never forget the time I visited a high-rise apartment building in nearby Dammam and shared an elevator with a Bedouin and four goats.

There is no doubt that things have radically changed since then, but this was a particular time and place. Driving felt otherworldly. A car in the left lane might suddenly swerve across traffic to turn right. Foreigners were invariably judged to be at fault in any collision. At night, vehicles would often be driven without headlights, presumably to conserve them. Passing on hills was common, and the shoulders of the road were littered with the husks of wrecked or burned-up cars. These were common scenes, although unlikely to be observed elsewhere.

Our assignments were long and repetitious—stretching from one to three months or more—dictated by the cost of coach airfare. There was no individual telephone service. On rare occasions, our home office arranged for our wives in the U.S. to gather and place a call to a Saudi public phone service center, where we shared private conversations aloud with everyone listening on both ends. Speaking with our children was impossible except by relay. Often, after these brief conversations, our wives were left sobbing. The experience scarred us permanently, as it no doubt does many military families. Still, we were earning a living while many others back in the States were just scraping by.

On our time off, we drank Saudi champagne—apple juice mixed with Perrier—and hit the streets. The spice market offered colorful, fragrant piles of spices in open bowls; shawarma stands sold delicious slices of roasted lamb wrapped in pita bread straight from the rotisserie. Merchants displayed bronze pots and coffee urns while others sold Bedouin woven goods. In the *souks*, one could find anything from clothing to gold jewelry by weight, regardless of the often intricate Indian or Italian craftmanship. Once, three of us discovered a stand selling comical fake leather, fleece-lined caps with earflaps. We each bought one, fastened the chin straps, and photographed ourselves wearing our "Chinese Commie pilot hats." Well, we had to do something to amuse ourselves. Once, with a friend, I drove north from Dhahran toward Ras Tanura, another huge drilling and residential site. We stopped by the roadside and got stuck in the sand. Fortunately, our vehicle carried pieces of plywood, which gave the rear wheels purchase and allowed us to move free. Nearby, we noticed unusual formations of sandy crystals and discovered large sand roses—clusters of gypsum barite, geometric crystals formed from hardened sand. At other times, we visited nearby Arab settlements, such as Al Hofuf, to see the town's ancient mud-walled fortifications. Life offered little diversion: no family, little entertainment, no movies, television, Internet, bookstores or newsstands.

As I advanced in the company, I was allowed to write proposals and help pursue opportunities. One of these involved a master plan and design services for a new community at Yanbu, near Saudi Arabia's west coast. Attending the interview with a senior partner, we arranged for a hotel driver to take us from Jeddah to the meeting at Yanbu, north of Jeddah, near the Red Sea. It was inadvisable for us to drive, as roadblocks near the holy city of Medina barred non-Muslims. About a third of the way on the trip, I noticed the driver struggling to stay awake. He admitted he had been partying the night before. I decided to drive the remainder of the way, heedless of roadblocks.

We made it, completed the interview, and got the job. Later, the Royal Commission asked us to present our final work on December 23. We worried that many expats would be returning home for Christmas and that we might have trouble getting back ourselves, but there was no denying our client's request. We flew to Jeddah, rented a Hertz, drove to Yanbu, and delivered our presentation that afternoon. All went well, and it looked as though we would catch our flight out that evening. However, as we were preparing to leave, the client's project representative asked us to stay and answer a few questions. From that point on, it was white knuckles all the way. When he finally let us go, dusk had fallen, and we leapt into the car and sped away.

By then, night had settled in, and the road ahead might have numerous hazards. Sure enough, we encountered trucks driving toward us without lights, cars racing to pass on hills, and others overtaking directly in our path. Then came a new delay: we had to return the rented car, but the parking lot and access roads were jammed with Muslims sleeping on the asphalt, waiting for buses to take them east to Mecca for *hadj*, the annual worldwide pilgrimage. With time running out, we carefully drove to Hertz, parked outside, threw the keys on the counter, and sprinted to the terminal—last ones to board our flight.

Our stopover in Heathrow fell on Christmas Eve. I stretched out across two lounge seats, set my alarm, and dozed until my flight was called—the notorious Pan Am 103, later bombed in 1988. I arrived in Austin that same evening, where my boys begged me to take them to the latest 007 movie with Roger Moore. I slept through it, but Christmas Day—my birthday—was the best ever.

A year earlier, while working at Aramco, I was again kept at work until the day before Christmas Eve. All westbound flights were fully booked, and the only flights available for me to return home for Christmas were first class, going east around the world—through Pakistan, Hong Kong, Tokyo, Chicago, and, finally, Austin. I needed prior authorization from the office in Austin, which, fortunately, was granted. The journey was exhausting; I worried constantly and did push-ups in the aisles to keep my head clear. The difficulties and hazards of working in the kingdom were offset by the chance to continue practicing my trade while absorbing something of a wildly different culture—one that would eventually be a world player, its economy built on oil, a petro-state. Years later, I would see the results of this evolution in Dubai.

CHAPTER 5

A Lucky Duck

In 1979, I was still the only person in a firm of more than six hundred qualified to do master planning. We had a business development agent in Asia looking for opportunities. He had befriended a Chinese Hong Kong brother and sister who respectively headed small civil engineering and interior design firms. At the time, Hong Kong was a British protectorate under British legal and business practices, and it thrived as an international financial and trade center. By contrast, China's economy was struggling, stifled by an insular political and legal system with little exposure to Western capital or business practices.

In Chinese culture, most business opportunities arise from *guanxi*—personal or business relationships. Through such connections, the brother and sister learned that the authorities in the People's Republic of China (PRC) proposed to develop a Special Economic Zone in a small rural village immediately north of Hong Kong, on the Chinese border, named Shenzhen. Its purpose was to provide land, tax incentives, cheap labor, and market access to attract Western business, manufacturing, and capital investments. As neither of the two Hong Kong firms had any capacity to undertake design and development work on the scale that required for such, they decided to seek out large Western firms as partners.

They chose our firm along with a large British civil engineering company. When our chief of new business development described the project to me, he handed me airline tickets and told me I was a "lucky duck." Thus began a series of courtship meetings and banquets in Hong

Kong, where, we, together with the Chinese representatives, could meet and size one another up. My quick trip became a long one. I returned home to wait for my multi-visit visa and to brief our principals, then I went back to Hong Kong to prepare for our forthcoming meetings across the border. As we crossed the border to China, we passed a line of armed guards, the equivalent of Marines. I was nervous; in 1979, it was still unusual for a private American to travel in the PRC. One of the Chinese representatives accompanying us from Hong Kong tried to sneak in contraband and was loudly berated by a customs' agent for embarrassing China in front of "our foreign friends."

Outside the train terminal, we were greeted by the village mayor, dressed in clothing that appeared as though it might have been bought eight years earlier at Goodwill. We piled into his car while our luggage followed in another vehicle. The mayor's car, I guessed, was a dusty, dented Mercedes-Benz about ten years old, with a driver behind the wheel. As we drove along, there was a big thump. We had hit a dog, but we didn't stop. We disembarked at a run-down hotel, likely the most luxurious in town, and were invited to dinner at six.

When my British engineer colleague and I arrived for dinner, we discovered that we were the only ones who spoke English. Neither of us spoke Mandarin, the standard language throughout China. In Hong Kong, the prevalent spoken language was Cantonese. We were shown to a table and, thankfully, seated next to each other. To break the ice, we were served glasses of mao-tai, a traditional and powerful liquor made of red sorghum—106 proof, with 53 percent alcohol by volume. Not for the faint of heart. Afterward, we were asked to take our seats, if sober enough to find them, and begin the meal.

From my time in Hong Kong, I was more or less used to what I might expect. Unfortunately, this banquet was meant to impress us, and to the Chinese, that meant strange delicacies—the more bizarre, the better, in their view. We tucked into fried chicken feet, deer tendons, and sea cucumbers, accompanied by more mao-tai. I figured that the idea was to get everybody drunk enough to eat the stuff.

The next day, we sat through several meetings, all conducted in Chinese. In the afternoon, after one long, intense argument followed by an equally long soliloquy, I asked our Hong Kong partner what was being said. He turned to me and said, "He says it's okay." The Brit and I were merely observers—window-dressing. The deal was being cut by our Hong Kong partner. When we took him to task over this, he promised to be more considerate, but the following day unfolded just the same. I told him we needed aerial photography, topographic mapping, demographic data, and facility programs. He responded that all the information was classified.

It was clear this was going nowhere, so we decided to leave the next morning. That evening, the Brit and I, who got along quite well, had dinner together in his room. We heard what sounded like gunfire out the window, to the south. Convinced that border guards were shooting at Chinese citizens trying to escape to Hong Kong—a well-known and documented phenomenon outside the PRC—we listened uneasily. When we asked about it the next morning, our hosts shrugged and said it was just fireworks. Sure.

I must pause here to say a few words about the Central Kingdom, or *Chung Kuo*, the traditional name for China. This ancient culture was brilliant, although they have long had many problems with governance. The people are intelligent, tough, determined, and talented yet can also be boorish, pushy, corrupt, and bigoted. When I first visited in 1979, the country was backward, poverty-stricken, and suspicious. Still, it must be admitted that they have come a long way, fast, against formidable odds. Today, they are leaders in medicine, scientific research, space exploration, quantum physics, and artificial intelligence. They lead the world in the production of electric vehicles. Yet they are also ruled under a ruthless, brutal regime that steals ideas and technology from other nations, threatens neighbors, and strives for dominance on the world stage. If they can only be admired grudgingly, they nonetheless earn respect. They are serious people. Meanwhile, as their purposeful and aggressive advances continue, our leaders spend their energy denying men access to girl's bathrooms.

The lead fizzled out, no doubt given to either a better-connected group or one willing to buy the work with bribes. I continued to work on numerous projects nearby Malaysia, where, thanks to our Asia business development agent, we were involved in designing the UMNO (ruling Malay) party's complex. The prime minister was Mahathir Mohammed, a member of the country's most powerful party, UMNO (United Malays National Organization). This work led to several unrelated master-planning projects, as Malaysia grew more and more developed.

On my first trip to Kuala Lumpur, I witnessed Thaipusam, a Tamil ceremony which followers of the Hindu god Murugan pierce their bodies with skewers and hooks from which they hang weighty objects. I also discovered a weed resembling milkweed that cringes within a three-foot radius when stepped on.

One of my projects there was planning a resort development at Bukit Fraser (Fraser's Hill). There were also urban mixed-use projects in Kuala Lumpur and new communities along the Strait of Malacca. Our local office attracted some strange characters. One was a mysterious Korean guy named Tom. He asked me if I had ever been to Malacca, a historic town on the coast of the Strait. I had not, so he offered to hire a taxi to drive us there. Along the way, we saw a dead motorcyclist who had just been hit by a car. It was grim. We arrived in Malacca, but I was still shaken by what we had seen. Nevertheless, we roamed around a little. On our return trip to Kuala Lumpur, Tom laid his hand on my leg and then moved it upward. I removed it, and not a word was said for the rest of the ride. The man who led our KL office later told me that he suspected Tom was a member of the Korean CIA. Weird! I met several other people, including an elderly Pakistani who spoke the Queen's English perfectly, and two sweet Chinese-Malaysian girls, named Jenny and Shi Pei, who worked as secretaries. They were very kind to me, and one of them later married and moved to Houston. We have recently exchanged Christmas greetings.

Prime Minister Mahathir's rival during this time was Anwar Ibrahim, a rising party member until Mahathir arranged his arrest and imprisonment on charges of sodomy (though Anwar was married then). In 2015, however, Anwar rejoined Mahathir in a new movement Mahathir had formed to regain leadership, which happened in 2018.

Betty and I moved to Houston from Austin when my firm was relocated, but we had already made friends with a couple from our former neighborhood who were former Aramcons. The wife, Juliette, was a Spanish lady who swore like a sailor and had a warm, outgoing demeanor. Her husband, Bill, was a member of the Petroleum Engineering Society, and was organizing a society tour to China in 1982. Naturally, we signed up as temporary members. Bill eventually gathered a group of ten, and once we secured our visas, we departed.

When we landed in Beijing, it was already dark although it was just eight o'clock and no other aircraft were visible. The airport terminal was dimly lit, and the empty news rack held no magazines or even newspapers. Juliette excused herself to use the toilet. When she emerged, she was cussing furiously. She told Betty she had sat on the sparkling white toilet seat, only to discover it was sticky with fresh paint. She tried to remove it but couldn't. We boarded a bus and departed for our hotel in the center of town. There was no traffic, only an occasional bike rider at intersections, illuminated by a single light bulb.

Exhausted, we went to bed and tried to sleep, although the room was stifling. We soon learned that the heat would remain on, regardless of the weather, until a mandated date. Afterward, no hotels had air conditioning. The bathroom floor drain emitted a nauseating stench. At breakfast, we met with our two guides—one a tour guide, the other a national caretaker from the Communist Party. We visited the Forbidden City, Temple of Heaven, Coal Hill, Summer Palace, Great Wall, and Ming Tombs. We had a strange welcome dinner, and I took morning runs in Tiananmen Square. Today, access to Tiananmen Square is tightly controlled by a regime that refuses to acknowledge the fact that their own government slaughtered hundreds, perhaps thousands, of young protesters there in 1989. In Hong Kong, the same regime now prevents residents from commemorating that massacre, as they once were free to do.

The daytime weather was smoggy, but there was minimal traffic. All the Chinese men and some women wore Mao suits. There was no clothing that could be mistaken for Western styles. A few days later, we left by a bus for Hangzhou. Along the way, we saw countless vegetable gardens, their plants sheltered beneath arches wrapped in plastic—exactly as we would later see in North Vietnam.

In Hangzhou, a renowned lakeside garden city, we checked into a waterfront hotel. By then, my clothing was becoming somewhat rancid, so I sent it to the hotel laundry. It was returned that afternoon, neatly folded and wrapped in paper—yet still sopping wet.

We left for Shanghai, where there was more activity. We stayed in what had been once the French ambassador's house, now converted to a tourist hotel. It was equipped with a television set, covered by a precious velvet cozy, obviously a luxury feature, though all broadcasts were in Mandarin. We visited the Bund, the old international settlement along the Huangpu River. While there, I was approached by friendly residents eager to practice their English. I should have been equally ambitious to learn Mandarin, but it wasn't a conducive environment for study.

From Shanghai, the traditional financial and business capital of China, we flew to Xinjiang Province, home of the Uyghur people, where we visited one of the very few mosques in the country. This was before the Uyghurs were ruthlessly repressed, imprisoned, and "reeducated" by the Party.

Next, we traveled by train to Xi'an, eager to see the famous terracotta soldiers. We were allotted one hour, although for the first forty minutes, we sat in a conference room while our Party guide delivered a harangue on the historic splendor of China, continued in modern times by the benevolent Communist Party. At last, with twenty minutes remaining, we were able to make a frenzied review of these masterpieces, each representing an individual member of Emperor Qin Shi Huang's personal guard. It was a breathtaking display. Near the hall where the excavated ranks of statues reside, lies a huge mound rumored to be the emperor's burial site. Legend holds that it contains a scale model of the then-known China, with silver rivers of mercury. Qin Shi Huang is respectfully remembered for unifying the warlord states, establishing a system of weights and measures, building the Great Wall, and standardizing the national language.

Eventually, we returned to Hong Kong's Kai Tak Airport, where airplanes typically approached with the left wing tilted upward, through a narrow corridor of apartments and laundry. We joked about whether we had snagged someone's pajamas. The weather was balmy once again.

CHAPTER 6

White Devils

In 1984, I was working back in the States, and we were in the throes of a deep recession. There were lots of cars from Michigan, easily identified by their black license plates, whose drivers had come south looking for work. But things got just as bad in Houston as well. People who couldn't pay their mortgages or their rent simply left their keys in the mailbox and walked away. Although I had been placed in charge of my firm's architecture, landscape architecture, and planning division, it was a thankless job, as I had to let go many of my friends and colleagues because the workload was shrinking rapidly.

As I thought about it, most of our work was real estate developer-driven, and they couldn't secure financing for new projects when demand was so low. We had little work in the public sector, having never pursued it, and like health-care work, it would take a long time to break into since we lacked experience. It seemed to me that our only potentially viable market was overseas. As the firm's founder put it, "You have to hunt where the ducks are," and there were none in our pond.

I decided to pursue more work in Asia, where opportunities still existed. I persuaded the senior principals to let me establish a new office in Hong Kong, where U.S. firms were showing strong interest in the potential Chinese market nearby. We began to probe prospective clients, and their responses were encouraging. We already had a small but highly visible interior design project in Hong Kong—the American Club, a social hub for Americans and other businessmen angling to find work in Southeast Asia. My firm's founder and I traveled to Hong

Kong to look for office space. We found some in Connaught Centre, a modern British-designed downtown building in Central (downtown), characterized by its uniformly round windows. Local Chinese referred to it as "the building of a thousand assholes." Later, one of my Houston colleagues would say that, with me there, it would be "the building of a thousand and one assholes."

In Hong Kong, buildings do not have fourth floor. The number 4 is considered unlucky, much as we often skip the thirteenth floors. Another cultural adjustment was the Chinese belief in *feng shui,* aimed at creating spaces that generate positive *chi,* or energy, for business and for life in general. There are also many ways to create negative *feng shui,* which is widely believed to bring harmful conditions. Thus, any proper Hong Kong building design or space layout required the services of a *feng shui* consultant to eliminate potentially negative conditions. For that reason, we were advised to relocate or reorient CEO offices according to the compass, regardless of the impact on efficiency or usefulness, and broom closets could become important spaces.

My family and I relocated in 1984, after finding housing in Repulse Bay, on the south side of the island, and enrolling our two teenage sons in high school. This marked the beginning of a successful three-year business venture. Although personally challenging, it was rewarding from a business standpoint and helped the firm in Houston make payroll more than once. Our work and opportunities grew throughout the region: Kuala Lumpur, Malaysia, Bangkok, Manila, and in Hong Kong. U.S. firms such as IBM and American Express were expanding in Asia while local firms were ill-prepared to design for American space standards or operating requirements. For the first time, Americans outnumbered Brits in Hong Kong.

We had arrived at an interesting time. As European, British, and American expatriates, we were all *gweilows* in Cantonese—"white devils." The British had long ruled Hong Kong, and its expat community remained socially dominant. My office employees were mostly locals, Hong Kongers who were generally content leading their own personal lives. But together with *gweilow* clients, other expats, and friends, we had an active business and social life—dinners, parties, and weekend cruises on Chinese junks or party boats. We heard about Vanna White, but at first, I thought it was the name of a toothpaste. One toothpaste carried the repulsive name *Darkie*, featuring a minstrel figure on its packaging. It may have originated from Australia. At Stanley market, we came across men's underwear branded *Dicks*, advertised with an incredible bulge and labeled as size "Largie." Breakfast cereal was scarce except in specialty markets. Hong Kongers preferred congee or rice porridge. Mexican restaurants were almost nonexistent, probably because cheese was not widely appreciated there.

We watched local television—*Miami Vice, Reilly: Ace of Spies*, and the hilarious *Blackadder* series. We played lots of mah-jongg. The mixture of nationalities (Hong Kongers were nominally British citizens) gave the city a distinct personality, and because Hong Kong adhered to the British legal standards, it remained stable and economically attractive. It was vibrant, with a busy, purposeful population, a democratic government, thriving business center, and an exciting mix of cultures. The weather was usually moderate to hot, and Christmas felt strange, with temperatures in the high eighties or nineties and the day treated as ordinary in the local culture.

I worked hard on new business development. Along the way, I encountered some pitfalls. I met a *gweilow* who seemed to have connections in China. He invited me to join him on a business development journey, first up the Pearl River from Hong Kong to Guangzhou. Next, we boarded a train to Shanghai. As with trains we had taken on during our 1982 trip, one could travel hard class (coach) or soft class (first). The cost difference was *de minimis,* so we traveled in relative comfort.

When we arrived in Shanghai, my friend claimed he had a contact who controlled government property on the Huangpu River above the Bund—the residential quarters of prerevolutionary diplomatic and major commercial operations. We checked into a major tourist hotel.

The next morning, we went up to the dining room. We were the only guests. The flooring consisted of uneven wooden planks. The waitress, who spoke very little English, took our orders of scrambled eggs, toast, and coffee. After a forty-five-minute wait, our cold toast arrived, followed half an hour later by cold eggs, and, finally after another forty minutes, by lukewarm coffee.

My friend's lead did not pan out, so we decided to fly back to Hong Kong. In those days, flight reservations were made by telex to the airline. Telex was the ubiquitous means of communication, both internationally and locally, with typists at one end and printing machines at the other, much like telegrams. We went to the telex office, a small room on the ground floor of a nearby building. It was packed full with would-be local travelers clamoring for the attention of a single operator. My friend, much larger than I am, had a better chance of plowing his way forward. He was able to make our reservations on a CAAC (China Airlines) flight back to Hong Kong.

In 1986, our office won the interior design competition for the Asian Development Bank in Manila. Delivering our proposal, we tried to land on the day Ferdinand Marcos was overthrown but were turned away. The following day, we managed to land, attended our interview, and were subsequently awarded the project. This required us to relocate a team from Houston to Manila.

Back in Houston, my firm was still suffering the effects of the recession that had driven me to move to Hong Kong. They had just laid off my good friend and mentor from our days in Saudi Arabia, Kirby. Kirby had made magnificent drawings of sights he observed on his travels. He had recently lived in Kuala Lumpur and had been in charge of our design team there, working on the recently completed UMNO Center. His skills weren't of value in Houston's downbeat economy, but I felt they were crucial for our Manila project. He assembled a top-notch team from the discards of our domestic work and moved with his wife, Vera, to Manila. In time, revenues from the project carried the firm in Houston through months of dark days.

Later that year, we took our boys to England and then to Paris. We saw the Tower of London, a grim reminder of bloody King Henry VIII, Madame Toussand's wax museum, and Churchill's wartime headquarters buried beneath London. I rented a Ford, a right-hand drive vehicle, and we set off for the Cotswolds. It was quaint and lovely. We watched the wedding of a young Prince Andrew to Fergie, live on television. Inspired by my friend Kirby, I started a sketchbook and recorded parts of the trip. We visited Stratford-upon-Avon and Warrick castle, and later, the Lake District.

After returning our rental car, we went to Paris, where we stayed in a hotel near the Opera. The boys, starved for cultural improvement, avidly watched anything on French TV despite not being able to understand the language. We visited Versailles and the Eiffel Tower, where I immediately got terrified by the height of the observation deck looming over the sprawling City of Light. I also made sketches of Mont-Saint-Michel.

On another excursion from Hong Kong in 1987, we took our son Alan to Nepal. Barry was scheduled to go soon with a school group. Before we left, we were given loads of prescription medications to ward off mosquito-borne illnesses. The doctor who advised our group must have been a hypochondriac himself. Landing in Kathmandu—after the animals were shooed off the runway—we encountered wondrous sights, including a giant prayer bell and monkey-infested temples. We trekked out of Pokhara with sherpas and flew near Mount Everest. We also traveled to Thailand, where Betty had her fortune told by a blind beggar who declared that she was a very kind man who would live a long life.

To compensate for our homesickness, we adapted by celebrating moon festivals and the Queen's Jubilee. Some Hong Kong businesses were flirting with the mainland, with which they shared cultural, linguistic, and, in many cases, family ties. This was the beginning of troubling tensions between the British and China.

In 1987, Margaret Thatcher's government agreed to the handover of Hong Kong to China in 1997. China, in turn, agreed to allow Hong Kong's government to remain independent for fifty years, until 2047—a promise it would later renege on. In 2020, China compelled the Hong Kong legislature to pass the national security law, effectively ending the island's independence. Knowing that China was more interested in political control than economic viability, I had a sinking feeling in 1987 that the "One Country, Two Systems" concept was doomed. Since then, the situation has devolved into a sickening stew of cruel and bloody repression, intolerance of expression, and a lack of secure refuge for Western and Hong Kong businesses. I grieve for the people of Hong Kong.

CHAPTER 7

Let Me Entertain You

We returned to the U.S. in 1987, but the economy remained stagnant. One afternoon two years later, back in Houston, I received a call from a well-known placement agency. They asked about my potential interest in working in France. A well-known entertainment company was developing a theme park just outside Paris. I thought about it for at least two seconds and asked, "When?"

They were looking for someone to manage the master planning process for the project, based in Paris. In Florida, I met with a Chinese American fellow about my age who was originally from China, later relocated to Hong Kong, and eventually became the company's worldwide head of master planning and architecture. I had respected him ever since seeing him give a presentation a few years back, and we hit it off immediately. This project required expertise in master planning, experience in real estate development, and familiarity with the field. The fact that I was also a licensed architect was a plus. I thought I had died and gone to heaven.

I was asked to come to Paris to meet with the vice president in charge of real estate development. I would be working directly with him and his team as well as the French planning authority while keeping the Florida master planning chief informed. It seemed like an ideal situation, and I was told I could expect to remain in that role for thirty years. However, there was one tiny problem: the head of HR in Paris wanted to try an experiment, and I was to be the guinea pig. I was designated a "local hire," subject to French taxes and paid in francs rather than dollars. I would need to find my own housing and pay the rent, secure a French driver's license, cover the cost of installing our kitchen and appliances, and learn French on my own. I was led to believe this was normal, and it was—for French employees. But I later learned that other U.S. employees brought to France by the company were subject to none of this. They were assisted in finding a fully furnished apartments, their rent was paid, they were reimbursed for taxes, and they received driving and language lessons. When I discovered this, I exploded. The company dug in its heels, and I would have quit and returned home were it not for the expense. Eventually, after I had proved my worth, they relented on some of these grievances. Still, the simmering ill will we felt when comparing our life to that of other company expatriates ultimately became intolerable.

I remained with the company for three years, which were rewarding in and of themselves. I loved living on the Left Bank in the 5th arondissement—going to the hardware store or the museum at my convenience, without having to pack a bag or catch a bus before I was finished getting to know a place. I got back to the U.S. frequently on business, sometimes twice in one week. The company eased the strain; I was able to fly first class or to downgrade to business class if Betty joined me. Executives were treated far more generously than I had ever experienced in consulting, where we flew only coach. Once, flying back to Paris from Los Angeles, my fellow passengers included Mel Brooks, Anne Bancroft, and Morley Safer.

We traveled extensively because my weekends were mostly free—visiting Belgium, England, Spain, Italy, Germany, Czechoslovakia, and even Kenya with friends. As an owner's representative, I learned about the other side of real estate projects from a developer's perspective rather than as a consultant. My French got better, and I grew able to take a broader view of current events. I learned to admire the French. They have endured much. They played a generous role in our revolution, although theirs followed ours in a bloody slaughter. Unlike us, who were settled by the British, they lived under Nazi rule. They do not appreciate foreigners who insist on speaking English rather than attempting French, who talk loudly in restaurants, or who otherwise behave boorishly. Nor do they enjoy listening to foreigners mangle their language. As Stanley Karnow describes in his book *Paris in the Fifties*, "The French were simultaneously sophisticated and parochial, methodical and anarchistic, individualistic and conformist, flexible and stubborn, liberal and antediluvian, prudent and rash, puritanical and wanton, logical and wildly irrational." I felt more positively, but he may have had a point.

In my sketchbook, I made drawings of Fontainebleau and Vaux-le-Vicomte, Place des Vosges, the view from our apartment over Boulevard Saint-Germain and Rue de Poissy, as well as dinners with guests and other moments.

Russian President Mikhail Gorbachev was presiding over the dissolution of the USSR and came to visit French President Francois Mitterrand at his home, a few blocks west of us off Boulevard Saint-Germaine, in the 5th arondissement, on the Left Bank. One afternoon at the Musee Carnavalet, I heard a distinctly recognizable voice behind me. Sure enough, it was the NBC Nightly News anchor Tom Brokow, commenting on a Picasso painting. Paris seemed to be an attractive destination for NBC.

One morning, Betty, longing for her life in America, happened upon a film crew shooting a segment with Willard Scott of the *Today's Show*. On screen he was affable, even playful, but he gave Betty a very cold shoulder. At the American University Women's group, Betty met a woman named Kathryn Altman, who turned out to be the wife of legendary American director Robert Altman. She and Betty grew close, and we were invited to a private screening of Altman's film *Vincent and Theo*—about Vincent van Gogh and his brother. The film wasn't ready for release and had no musical soundtrack. We came away realizing how important a score can be for any film.

Sometimes things got a little uncomfortable. One evening, when the American chairman of our company visited us along with other U.S. dignitaries, we gathered for an outdoor banquet in the Bois de Boulogne. Long speeches and toasts rolled by, and the word *synergy* was mentioned positively at least four hundred times. Then came the food—course after course after course—and we began to feel like we were being stuffed like geese to make pate' of our livers. At the time, the Bois was known primarily as a place inhabited by hookers and drag queens at night. It made me think of another evening in the Bois.

In 1966, we had spent the morning visiting the Chapelle Le Ronchamp by Le Corbusier in France and then driving west to Paris on our Vespa. There were no autoroutes or six-lane highways. In the idyllic countryside, a bee flew under my helmet. There were a few nervous moments as I tried to lift my helmet and steer the Vespa. The youth grapevine had told us to camp in the Bois de Boulogne, where there was a campsite with facilities. We crossed to the west side, where it was located, found it, pitched our tent, and unloaded the gear that we had bought a month earlier in Vienna.

Several other tents were nearby, one occupied by Stephan and Karen, whom we had met on Crete in Mattala. They were still doing their hashish thing, so we didn't talk for long. A big, tough-looking guard with a shaved head, wearing a leather overcoat, looked for all the world exactly like a Gestapo goon. We steered away from him. We picked up a *Time* magazine someone had left and learned that a young man named Charles Whitman had just conducted two mass murders in Austin, Texas, and at the University of Texas tower. It was the first mass shooting in America that we were aware of, and it marked the beginning of a series of gun-inflicted massacres that continue to this day.

Later, we were still in Paris when Germany reunited, and soon we saw east Europeans, formerly part of the Soviet empire, begin to arrive on tour buses. These refugees apparently wanted to see what the West was like, but few had valid currency. We spotted dozens of them sleeping under shrubs in parks and trying to rest on metro benches in subway stations, only to be shooed away by guards. I felt a kinship with these vagabonds.

We tend to entertain visions of ourselves that may not coincide with the perceptions of others. As a result, decision-makers in one culture can often misunderstand the cultures they interact with. For example, when my firm planned a visit for French officials to see our American operation, the Americans decided to include a presentation of "living statues"—real humans painted uniformly with a color who stood absolutely still. Yes, France adored its great mime Marcel Marceau, who used his art to explore and express humanity without speech; but what would they make of the living statues? Most of them were appalled. After some years living in France, I suspected our guests would be repulsed by these intensely inhuman representations, with their stifling of human traits, as opposed to Marceau's art which was active, expressive, and emotionally appealing. Meanwhile, our U.S. counterparts thought they had hit a home run.

Our son Barry had enrolled in a self-directed curriculum at Evergreen University in Washington state. While visiting us in Paris, he embarked on an essay about the German occupation in France. He hoped to interview Parisians about their wartime experiences. We advised him to modify his plan and not to sit down next to a random stranger in the Jardin de Luxemburg, asking about this painful period. Although Europe, particularly France, was psychologically damaged by World War II, France and Italy have cultures particularly notable for living in the present, savoring the experiences and customs of everyday life.

We convinced him to begin with our friends after first discussing the matter with them. He interviewed Monsieur Patel, an elderly attorney who lived on the floor above us, who had visited the U.S. as a young man, was a member of an Olympics rowing team, and spoke good English. He also interviewed a lady friend of ours that Betty met through the American Women's Group, a painter. Barry attempted these interviews in French and did a commendable job. A year later, he moved to France after spending a summer in Alicante, Spain. He enrolled at Paul Valery University in Montpellier, in the south of France. Soon, we had visitors his age who would show up at our doorstep announcing, "Barry sent me."

Our older son, Alan, had joined the U.S. Air Force and by chance was stationed at the Royal Air Force Base in Alconbury, England. Because the boys and I had been early adopters of personal computers, his background suited him for information technology in an intelligence unit there, where he also learned a variety of software languages that would help him later in life. A further benefit was the USAF Base Exchange where he could buy U.S. groceries and other products at a steep discount. We took the English Channel ferry to Dover, joined him for a weekend, and loaded up on American goods at the BX—items otherwise unavailable in France.

It had been several years since I had driven in the United Kingdom, and this time it was in a left-hand-drive French company car. I managed fairly well driving on the right; I had done so in Hong Kong in the eighties and previously in the sixties on our Vespa motor scooter. In 1966, just outside London, Betty and I were nearing town on the motorway in heavy traffic on a rainy afternoon when I skidded and tipped over, finding myself under the Vespa. Betty landed beside me, sitting on the motorway macadam, holding her purse in her lap. It was a miracle that we both survived.

In 1990, we traveled with a friend, a Czech expat, from Paris to Prague. The Iron Curtain had just been lifted, but all the shops had empty window displays. In Prague's Old Town Square, a man set up a suitcase on a stand and offered beautiful crystal goblets for next to nothing. When he sold out, another entrepreneur appeared with his own suitcase. We heard that Japanese tourists were buying chandeliers. That evening, we went to a magic lantern performance where tickets cost only one dollar each. The next day, Pope John Paul II held a mass across the Danube from the square, and there were yellow streamers everywhere. In the square, a public microphone and speakers remained from the previous authorities, who had used them to harangue citizens. We visited Konopiste Castle, where Archduke Franz Ferdinand had displayed an impressive array of deer antlers. Later, it became interesting to reflect on these experiences in the context of modern Europe.

In 1991, we went on a second journey, arranged by our Czech friend, to Kenya. Our guide, Francis, came from a low-status tribe but was a wonderful companion. Our first stop was the Amboseli, where we saw herds of zebra and elephants, along with hordes of monkeys that swarmed the outdoor breakfast area, attempting to snatch food away from tourists. The camp had hired a Maasai gentleman to chase them off with a stick and a slingshot. He was kept very busy. To the south, across the veldt, rose Mount Kilimanjaro. Later, we traveled north, to the Masa Mara, where we observed lions, hippos, and cheetahs. I signed up for my first balloon ride over the Serengeti and marveled as we floated above massive herds of wildebeests before landing beside a Maasai village.

Meanwhile, back in Paris, our team of expats, Europeans, and locals were working feverishly toward opening day on April 2, 1992. The landscaping team was sorely frustrated when, no sooner had they covered areas with show displays of plants, local residents would arrive at night and carry them off. Although Zoom had not yet been invented, the company had established a similar video and audio connection between the development team in Paris and management in California. We could discuss issues in real time, share diagrams, and see the people we were speaking with— usually the chairman. Studio executives also visited, primarily focused on designing guest experiences, along with our chief U.S. real estate development leader, with whom we conducted feasibility studies and addressed other challenges related to building such a massive project. My role was leading a small team that interfaced the French development authorities, managing U.S. and other consultants involved with infrastructure and planning, and coordinating with facility design and development teams. It was an enormously complicated project, made more difficult by the egos of many highly intelligent, strong-willed company veterans. Everyone had strong opinions about everything, and only the chairman, consulting with his closest advisors, could reconcile disagreements.

This was when the U.S. launched "Desert Storm," the first Gulf War. We watched the real-time broadcasts of the aircraft strikes on French television. Even Walter Cronkite was speaking dubbed French. Air travel became nonexistent, as we were all unsure if it was safe. One group of consultants found themselves completely alone on their flight to France, and everyone became fearful of flying on U.S.-based airlines.

Some of our American consultants behaved badly. One tried to play politics, trying to stoke relationships within the company's U.S. hierarchy to bypass us, their direct client. They soon learned that strategy did not work. They tried to charge us for private limo rides on the way from home to the airport, and one principal brought her husband to Paris and attempted to bill us for his trip, although he had no role in the project. I later discovered that the same consultants once had an appointment in Dallas at EDS to propose a project to H. Ross Perot. They arrived in a fleet of limos. Perot looked out the window, seeing them arrive, and allegedly said, "Let 'em unload and drag their butts on up here, and then tell 'em we no longer want their services." Interestingly, Perot kept a small museum at the entrance to his office displaying gear from his 1979 rescue of two EDS employees from an Iranian prison, the basis for the book and film *On the Wings of Eagles*.

Another consultant failed to realize they were on a hot mic when they launched into a derogatory monologue about our company after having worked on one of our projects. One noted architect, a fellow in the American Institute of Architects, called my apartment in Paris and made drunken remarks to my son who had answered the phone. We might have chalked it up to jet lag, but we held ourselves to a much higher standard and expected the same of our consultants.

Opening day at the project in 1992 was literally sensational. Hollywood stars and well-known music groups flown in along with their retinues. It was an incredible series of performances, which we understood were broadcast live to the U.S. So now what? I could no longer accept the idea of living in France in my position for thirty years. I hoped to return to the U.S. and continue working with the company, but they had no reason to keep me on.

In June, we returned to Houston. After we landed, I saw pickup trucks on the road with rifle racks in the rear windows and felt we had made a dreadful mistake coming back.

CHAPTER 8

Back in the USA

We had been allowed to make a trip back to Houston to prepare for our return. Luckily, we found our home. I had no prospects and struck out on my own—literally struck out. After a few disquieting months, my first client saw a news article about my recent background and decided to give me a try. His idea was to build a dog racetrack south of Houston. I was grateful but had little idea of what a racetrack entailed, but that didn't deter him. He was a character, and I instantly liked him, although he puzzled me. An heir of family interests, he led a title company and a petroleum company until his death in 1995. He wore white linen suits and a straw hat. He was a lawyer and a former platoon leader in Korea and served one term in the Texas House of Representatives. He used to ski Aspen in leather shorts and boots. He even ran for the U.S. Senate, promising he wouldn't stay in office long because he was likely to die soon. He kept his promise, unfortunately.

Another friend, Frank, had a contact with a reportedly former CIA agent who maintained connections in Manila and asked me to join his team. We were chosen to develop feasibility studies, a program, and a plan for a Philippine Exposition in 1998 at the former Clark Air Force Base outside of Manila. The concept originated with one of the Philippine senators, which we imagined would guarantee its successful development.

On arrival at Manila International Airport, I expected to be picked up by a car arranged by our client. I waited and waited, but no car appeared. A guy about seventy yards away offered me a ride, yet I was wary having heard tales of arriving passengers taken to remote spots and robbed—or worse. I refused until it was clear something had gone wrong with the arrangements. Gritting my teeth, I approached him. He didn't have a taxi but a regular car. I told him where I was going, and we agreed on a price before setting off. Then the driver said he had to pick up someone else, another Filipino. I was extremely nervous but stayed seated when another man slid into the front seat, and we drove on. I turned to the driver and said, "Look, I'm here to see the sights, and I don't have a car and driver yet. Do you think you could help me?" He said he could, and I asked for his card. "We can talk about the price tomorrow," I added. He took me straight to my hotel, and I breathed a sigh of relief. I have no idea if my fears were justified, but I vowed never to expose myself that way again—until I did, later.

We stayed in Makati, an upscale retail and hotel center in Manila, where we also worked. Clark field was abandoned by the U.S. after being inundated with volcanic ash from the eruption of Mount Pinatubo in 1991. We formed a team with varied backgrounds—exposition design, market and financial feasibility, architectural design and master planning. When we visited Clark, we found a residential area with ash piled up to the windowsills and flew over the Pinatubo crater. I couldn't help but think of Pompeii. There was an array of tall antennae in a level area which became the focus of our concepts. Manila itself had changed little since the days we had worked on the Asian Development Bank. Jeepneys, highly decorated transit vehicles used as minibuses, were everywhere. We visited antique shops and stores offering specialty baskets and other décor. I shopped for personalized cigar boxes made of Nara wood, embellished with recipients' names in flowing calligraphy, and found a statue of Santa Claus riding a large pig. The project went nowhere.

Eventually, I grew weary of trying to market my skills alone. As a one-man shop, marketing interfered with my work and vice-versa. And although I had managed to save some money from my past projects, we didn't have enough to secure our future. Fortunately, another friend, who was picked to head the Houston branch of a national firm of architects, planners, and designers, decided to make me an offer. He wanted my help to transform the primarily interior design firm into an architectural powerhouse. I joined, and before long, we had succeeded in building the largest, most diverse and capable design firm in the nation. The firm was exceptionally well run, and employees were granted stakes in our success, so their efforts paid tangible dividends. The leaders demanded excellence, dedication—and got groundbreaking performance.

Eventually, we began to be considered for international projects. In 2003 and 2004, I led the design of a large Australian oil company's headquarters building in Port of Spain, Trinidad, which in turn led to other local projects. I responded to a request for proposals for the design and planning of a huge mixed-use development in Dubai, which would become the Emirate's International Finance Center. Knowing what our prospective clients expected, we not only prepared a written proposal but also a physical model to explain our design ideas. We won the project, which led to numerous others in the Middle East. First, we refined the master plan, illustrating our concepts with 3D computer modeling. We studied comparable developments, such as Las Ramblas in Barcelona, to provide conceptual examples. Next, we created staging plans so the project's components could be built in phases. More refined physical models followed, along with detailed renderings of various features. We considered issues such as underground parking because of Dubai's withering heat, shaded and covered walkways, utilities routing, access routes, and viable land uses. It stretched us, yet we welcomed the challenge.

As we worked in Dubai, I was mindful of its next-door neighbor, Saudi Arabia, and my experiences there. The climate was the same, miserably blistering hot in the daytime. Dubai had more tolerant rules than Saudi Arabia; alcoholic beverages were available to foreigners. To my ear, which was not reliably trained, the spoken and written language seemed identical.

Both the United Arab Emirates (UAE) and the kingdom are Islamic nations, and men in both wear the same white robes, headwear or *ghutras* held in place by a black *agal*, or headband. Businessmen are instantly recognizable by their starched crisp linens. Women's dress is similar, with black *abbahs* from head to toe, although many Lebanese women there wear jeans and colorful tops. Prayers to Allah are offered five times a day. During Ramadan, Arabs do not eat in the daytime.

I observed the fasting during business meetings, and that evening, my rice and mushroom soup was the best meal I had ever tasted.

Dubai is known for its modern monuments: the Burj al Khalifa tower, at 428 meters (1,400 feet) is currently the tallest structure on earth. The city also boasts three man-made islands—Palm Jumeirah, Palm Jebel Ali, and Palm Deira. Saudi Arabia is attempting to build a vast new high- tech megacity on its western coast, Neom. Following the footsteps of the ancient Egyptians, these projects resemble the Pyramids in their audacity and their quest for enduring world significance. It's worthwhile to compare them with the artifacts of ancient Greece, Rome, or Angkor Wat, considering their rationale, cost, and historical weight.

I spent the last several years working on projects of that kind, together with domestic work on mixed-use developments, hotels, and convention centers. However, the firm was not immune from turf battles and power intrigues among ambitious colleagues. I had grown tired of using my skills to make wealthy groups or individuals wealthier. I decided it was time for a change. I finally chose to pursue painting as a second career and enrolled in the exceptional Glassell School Art at Houston Museum of Fine Arts. While still employed part time, I studied there for more than three years, learning the rudiments of painting. It was rewarding, and I enjoyed meeting others who were also drawn to art. I began working on figurative or representational forms, infused with abstract, painterly, and even surreal elements. The closest examples would be works by René Magritte or, ideally, Gerhardt Richter. I loved being able to express myself through this work. Though by no means masterful, I was skilled enough to gain recognition.

CHAPTER 9

Fresh Start

Although I had retired as a partner in my firm, I continued working as a consultant for another Atlanta company. This second firm had developed close working relationships with a well-placed Dubai developer who had access to enormous financial resources.

Through this connection, we received a lead—probably from our UAE clients—about a new resort community planned just outside Almaty, Kazakhstan. We insisted on an upfront payment to cover expenses and were surprised when they agreed and sent it. In January, I flew to Almaty, a city I had never visited. The trip from the airport to the hotel presented a challenge similar to one I had experienced in the Philippines. Almaty is notorious as a place wherein arriving air passengers are taken to remote areas and threatened if they refuse to hand over their cash and credit cards. Again, I somehow managed to escape that danger.

We met with our client's representative, a straightforward Russian woman who spoke good English. It turned out that the proposed resort was a pet project of President Nursultan Nazarbayev's family, and one of our tasks was to find an appropriate place for his compound and villa. The project was also to be remotely overseen by the president's billionaire daughters and sons-in-law. It was to be another kind of self-satisfying monument to power.

Taking the lead from my colleague, a vice president of the second firm, we went to the hotel spa for a massage. I had never experienced anything like it. The masseuses were Russian women, tough as nails.

For half an hour she beat me on my back, shoulders, buttocks, and legs, causing my nose to expel copious amounts of what were said to be poisons. Finally, I removed my underwear and stepped into an icy shower, thinking I would surely suffer frostbite. Afterward, the sense of physical well-being was almost overwhelming.

Later, while exploring Almaty, we came upon a park where artists displayed oil paintings of nature scenes. We saw brilliant yellow cathedrals, startlingly contrasted against the surrounding fields of snow. We watched a wedding party, the groom posed for photos crouching with open arms, carrying a bouquet in his right hand. He was comically replicating the monumental Soviet-styled, blackened bronze statue behind him—the 28 Panfilov Guardsmen who had stopped the advance of fascist tanks in World War II. The enormous leading figure crouched with spread arms, a pair of grenades in his right hand.

Back at the hotel, we sketched out a detailed concept and presented it to our Russian female client. What happened after that, we'll never know.

In 2007, that developer was invited by the government of Vietnam to conduct a feasibility study for the development of Phu Yen Province, an area of more than 1,940 square miles. I led the new firm's team in assessing the attributes of the region, exploring potential drawbacks, considering appropriate land uses and describing their interrelationships, and recommending implementation steps. We met with government officials to understand their objectives, visited the huge site to evaluate conditions, made notes of external factors such as transportation and skilled labor availability, and prepared lists of proposed locations for various land uses. Then we explored concepts to integrate all this information, proposing optional arrangements and evaluating their pros and cons.

Our study was well-received by Vietnamese agencies; however, our Dubai client faced troubling business headwinds and ultimately decided not to pursue the project. Although local authorities have implemented some of our recommendations, they lack the massive capital necessary to carry them out fully.

Betty and I later visited Vietnam. On my previous trip, I had not gone into North Vietnam. This time we first went to Hanoi, where I saw the lake where John McCain's aircraft went down during the Vietnam War. Along the shore, further around the lake, there were paddleboats in the shape of swans. A bit later, we took a taxi to the Hanoi Hilton, where American prisoners, including McCain, had been held. We saw the cell where he had been suspended by his thumbs. McCain, the son of an American Navy admiral, was badly mistreated. Years later, Donald Trump, who evaded military service, remarked of McCain: "I like people that weren't captured."

We traveled the length of Vietnam, stopping by Hoa An, Pleiku, Da Nang, and ending in Saigon, or Ho Chi Minh City. I left convinced that invading Vietnam was one of the most serious mistakes our country ever made. There is no residual anger against Americans, although we deserve it. These people had been fighting a revolution against the French, and then we piled on for no good reason. They still bear the horrible scars from our bombs, napalm, and other inhuman actions. There was a terrible misconception on our part during the war that communism there would endanger us if we allowed it to survive. When they defeated us, they later proved that assumption to be completely wrong. What a waste of human life, energy, and wealth—resources that could have been used for constructive efforts, along with our precious honor and ideals. And now, it seems we are repeating the same mistake, this time for oil, as in Iraq and Venezuela, or for unclear reasons, as in Iran.

Traveling in two countries with Communist pasts, I observed certain similarities: The governing regimes of both are rigid, doctrinaire, and prone to punish those perceived to be threats to their authority. Kazakhstan has oil reserves while Vietnam has rare earth minerals, but neither has a robust economy. Vietnam is pursuing a similar path to China, attracting manufacturing with cheap labor and a stable economy.

Kazakhstan, on the other hand, follows the Russian model, maintaining a close grip on its oil supplies and using the revenues to benefit rulers, their families, and friends.

In Cambodia, we visited Angkor Wat—the largest religious complex in the world, first Hindu and later Buddhist. Built in the early twelfth century, it is a characteristic example of the Khmer unified architectural vocabulary. The site is surrounded by other abandoned temples, featuring gigantic carved stone heads.

The Khmer empire encompassed Cambodia as well as large portions of Thailand, Vietnam, and Laos. It was an empire based on conquest. I first learned about Cambodia during the Vietnam War, when Nixon's decision to bomb Laos in 1969 and Cambodia in 1970 was concealed from the American public. The administration attempted to block Hanoi's use of these previously uninvolved countries, through which the Ho Chi Minh Trail supplied and reinforced Hanoi's operations in South Vietnam. At the time, Cambodia's government, led by Prince Norodom Sihanouk, was becoming increasingly unstable and was soon toppled by the vicious and murderous Khmer Rouge regime.

That had largely faded away when we arrived, although the government remained somewhat unstable. I had never thought much about the Khmer Empire, although I was aware of Angkor Wat. While there, I saw the enormous reservoirs, moats, and channels surrounding the temple. Curious about them, I learned that they were there to create hydrostatic pressure that served as counterweight to allow the region's sandy soil to support the weight of the huge structures. They also served as catchment basins and sources of irrigation for surrounding farmland. This eventually led to a centralized system of governance and control to manage the ebb and flow of water throughout the monsoon seasons. Although the prevailing religion evolved from Hinduism to Buddhism, and successive wars and other events brought changes in governance, none deviated substantially from this centralized model.

As a result, the prevailing architectural style of the region's monuments was readily identifiable and usually incorporated fine examples of stonework. It was a hydraulic empire, shaped by natural conditions that demanded the control of water resources. Such control required long periods of stability that could only be guaranteed by conquest, as opposed to feudal societies in the West, which allowed more diversity without such powerful natural conditions.

CHAPTER 10

Independent Travel

We had traveled in pre-Maastricht Europe. The European Union is possibly the most important development in human civilization since the American Revolution. As a result, the word *Europe* carries far greater resonance today.

Friends from my college days suggested traveling in Argentina, and we agreed immediately. Our fair proficiency in Spanish proved highly useful. Together with a local travel agency, we mapped out an independent itinerary and identified reliable hotels, beginning in Buenos Aires. We settled into our hotel in Recoleta and used it as a base while getting familiar with the city on our own. One of our first stops was the cemetery, with its highly decorated tombs reminiscent of Père Lachaise in Paris. As Paris has its Jim Morrison tomb, with messages of love and longing for him, Recoleta has the tomb of Eva Duarte Peron, wife of Argentina's former dictator Juan Peron, and the subject of the play Evita, with its doleful song, "Don't Cry for me Argentina."

Buenos Aires was a great place to start. We visited the "Pink Palace," their version of the White House, where the "women in white," *Las Mujeres en Blanco,* still protest for women's rights and those who went missing under Argentina's dictatorship from 1976 to 1983. We attended a meal and tango performance, after which guests from many countries were acknowledged and asked to stand up. As George W. Bush was then America's president, deeply unpopular in Argentina and many countries, we were not acknowledged. Traveling south to Patagonia, where it got colder and colder, we arrived in El Calafate and visited the

Perito Moreno Glacier. We climbed part of the glacier and watched it calve fresh icebergs.

On a second trip, we returned to the same hotel in Buenos Aires. At the same tango show, there was still no acknowledgement of *los yanquis*. This time, we went north to Bariloche, a popular ski resort; although it was summer, the scenery was beautiful. We wanted to fly to Salta, in northern Argentina, but the air traffic controllers were on strike. We considered buses and rental cars, but the distances were too great.

Suddenly, the strike was over, and we got back to Buenos Aires before continuing on to Salta, a historic town in the north. Along the way, we drove across the Salinas Grande, a giant salt lake with no map or road markings. By the seat of our pants, we kept driving northward until finally, we made it to Salta.

In Salta, we discovered the Museum of High-Altitude Archaeology, which preserves the mummified remains of two young girls and a young woman from the Inca period. They were found in high altitude caves, together with artifacts from their time. It is believed that they were human sacrifices meant to appease gods of a nearby volcano on the Bolivian border. The cold, dry conditions kept them in a near-perfect state of preservation.

From Salta, we journeyed north toward the Bolivian border on a one-lane mountain trail that hugged the cliff face with few turnouts. We climbed to the pass at Cuesta de Lipán at 23,830 feet above sea level and continued down to the quaint village of Iruya, where we found spectacular views, traditional architecture, a quaint hotel, and a peaceful ambience. We joked that the directions to our hotel should have been "When you get to the second sleeping dog, turn left."

In 2008, we were invited by a friend to join a group her son was organizing to visit India. He was starting a "gap year" travel program for high school graduates and college students who wanted to pause their studies. We were to be his guinea pigs. This time, we traveled throughout northern India, beginning briefly in Delhi before going on to Kajurahu, Varanasi, and Agra. We saw the Taj Mahal; visited Buddhist shrines and temples; bathed our feet and surrendered our shoes and belts before entering a Jain bird hospital; visited a Hindu shrine to Ganesh, the elephant-headed god; viewed the erotic statues at Khajuraho; and explored Varanasi—the sacred city on the Ganges River.

Varanasi, previously referred as Benares, is a sacred site where the bodies of Hindus are cremated by the river. Upstream, clothed worshippers gather to bathe in the muddy waters. The stairs leading down to the river from the town above are called *ghats*. There are fires, snake charmers, and sightseeing boats. At night, candlelit waterfront spectacles draw crowds of visitors. In the town above, we saw a rickshaw driver—an untouchable—accidentally run a bike tire over the toe of a well-dressed businessman, who immediately slapped the poor man loudly across the face. The rickshaw driver simply cringed and took it as his due. If someone tells you that the caste system in India is now dead, they are misinformed.

Talk about an income gap. The daily life of most of India's citizens is wretched and desperate while the tiny mogul class rides above it all, floating on clouds of Bollywood movies, real estate, oil fields, government posts, and high-tech, riding in Mercedes limos. Yet many of these higher-caste, educated, and whip-smart people have come to America seeking opportunities. In doing so, they have enriched our economy and culture, leading some of our most important companies and employing many of our native-born.

I helped the second firm explore opportunities in Mumbai, India. They had established a relationship with a major conglomerate, and we traveled there to consider the possibilities for development. I had not previously been to Mumbai and was shocked, as we drove to our hotel in the evening, to see forms of sleeping people covering the sidewalks, some even encroaching in the roadway. The following day, we drove to the client's office, evading hordes of tuk-tuks along the way. We discussed services relating to the Bandra Kurla Complex, but ultimately the discussions went nowhere.

My friend Ed and I decided to visit Nepal. Traveling there through New Delhi, we soon arrived in Kathmandu. Wandering the streets, we encountered many exotic people, costumes, and practices. In Durbar Square, we saw the living goddess, the Kumari child princess Bhrikuti, embodying divine purity and worshipped by Hindus and Buddhists alike. We saw scores of lighted candles neatly ranked in rows along the sidewalks, symbolizing a religious practice unfamiliar to us. We visited the Monkey Temple, along with other temples and stupas.

From Kathmandu, we flew to Pokhara and embarked on a modest trek through jungle trails, across hanging bridges over mountain streams, before settling into our base camp.

From there, we hiked through mountain villages, passed water buffaloes, and visited a remote elementary school where kids had to hike two miles or more to attend classes. On one narrow, rocky mountain trail, we encountered runners training for a marathon. As a runner myself who had trained for marathons, I admired their deftness.

Next, we went to an open area with a river flowing through it to ride elephants. Each of us— Ed, I, and the others—managed to climb aboard these huge creatures, accompanied by a *mahout*, or elephant driver. We lumbered across the river and crashed through the brushy grassland on the other side. Suddenly, Ed's elephant, which was ahead of mine, stopped and refused to move. The *mahout* whacked its head, but to no avail. He finally got down and looked at the area where Ed's elephant was poking its trunk. There, he found Ed's clip-on plastic sunglasses, which had fallen from his shirt pocket. It was almost unbelievable that the elephant had heard the light clip-ons drop into the deep brush. Continuing, we saw rhinos, birds, and other wildlife, as well as termite mounds. When we returned, the elephants happily rolled in the river and sprayed water with their trunks.

A few days later, it was time to return home. In Kathmandu, one of the group members realized he had left something behind at the camp. Our guide, who was exceedingly accommodating, agreed to track it down. The next day, FedEx delivered it back to him. We were shocked to realize that our guide went to such trouble to retrieve nothing but a big wooden stick the fellow had picked up along a trail and used for walking.

Betty and I embarked on an excursion in Russia, beginning in Moscow and traveling to St. Petersburg in 2012, before the recent tensions. I had gone ahead to serve on a panel in Budapest to discuss transportation and was to meet her in Paris, where we would continue on to Sheremetyevo Airport. From Budapest, I had a tight connection in Frankfurt, and my bag didn't make it.

However, we found Moscow to be fascinating. We visited Red Square, where actors dressed as Putin and Stalin mingled with the crowd. We saw goose-stepping soldiers, the GUM department store, Lenin's Tomb, and the onion-domed cathedrals. To change dollars for rubles, we went to a bank exchange office with two other tour group members, John and Karla. There was a long line to enter a vestibule where a single teller worked. When we were next in line, a big tough man shouldered us aside and took our place. John said in English, "Excuse me, but we were here before you." The guy looked at us coldly and replied, "I don't wait!" After finishing his transaction, he returned to the waiting room and flipped the bird to Karla and Betty. I had the impression he was a Russian mafia, but disturbingly, he might not have been.

I was able to retrieve my bag from Lufthansa at Vnukovo Airport, taking the Moscow subway. I saw the embellished stations, including one where a bronze statue of a wolf or dog stood with a shiny nose. It was evidently irresistible to pass the statue without rubbing its nose. The subway car was crowded with people returning home, poking at their cell phones. It might as well have been New York. From Moscow, we traveled by boat toward St. Petersburg (nee Leningrad), through the canals Stalin had built with slave labor.

Along the way, we visited Kishi Island, where we saw the church made of cedar shingles. We met one of the shingle craftsmen and noticed he was missing a digit. Passing through Lake Ladoga, we arrived in St. Petersburg and stayed on the boat. A highlight for me was our visit to the Winter Palace, where the top floor houses some of the finest Impressionist paintings. We had not been informed about the gallery, but fortunately, I had read about it, and the works were enthralling.

The Soviet Union still lives in the minds of many Russians. So does the KGB, now called the FSB. Most people we encountered in Russia were likable, although many were wary or displayed animus. However, the dogmatic regime coddles oligarchs while permitting a modest level of financial stability for the general public. At a Moscow bus stop, I saw a well-dressed homeless woman sleeping on plastic bags of refuse. The memory became my oil painting, called Pink Lady.

In St. Petersburg, at the Church of the Spilled Blood in 2012, I saw a small group of young people erect a wooden cross bearing a young woman bound with cloth. A banner I later translated read: "Here is our democracy." In less than a minute, the youths were arrested by a swarm of police, and the cross was removed.

Afterward, we went to Estonia. Leaving the Russian border, we were told to disembark our bus and to pick up a suitcase, any suitcase, before approaching the Russian border control. We were also warned not to smile when presenting our passport to the border agents. Meanwhile, behind us stretched a line of trucks waiting to clear customs. We explored the old town of Tallinn and visited the Kumu Art Museum, one of the largest museums in Estonia and one of the largest art museums in Northern Europe. The main collection covers Estonian art from the eighteenth century onward, including works from the occupations period (1940–1991) that show both socialist realism and what was then Nonconformist art.

Socialist realism was usually devoid of complex artistic meaning or interpretation. It attempted to limit popular culture to a specific, highly regulated faction of emotional expression that promoted Soviet ideals.

As a "movement," nonconformist art was stylistically diverse. However, in the post-thaw era, its function and role in society became clear. The contrast between the two was interesting because many of the social realism painters were often excellent craftsmen, yet their work had almost no artistic or intellectual merit. It was fun to see the sense of liberation and humor in the artworks that emerged as the Soviets began to lose their grip. One could see the same dichotomy in other former satellite states. For instance, in the former East Berlin, a youthful *avant-garde* remains solidly entrenched in the art world, breaking norms and barriers.

To celebrate our fiftieth anniversary in 2013, we took our son Alan, who was divorced, and his three boys to Tanzania, traveling via Amsterdam. Our principal purpose was to expose our grandsons to a wider world. Our daughter-in-law Karen did not enjoy the thought of going to Africa, so we planned a different trip for our son Barry and his family.

We arrived in Amsterdam and stayed near Schiphol Airport. Taking the tram into town, we first enjoyed a canal cruise and then took Alan and the boys to Anne Frank's house. Fortunately, I had read about getting advance tickets online, and we were able to skip directly to the entrance. It was the first time that any of us had visited there, and it was chilling to see how that family almost survived the war. Afterward, we had coffee and sodas across the street from a marijuana café. Next, we went to the Rijksmuseum, where we saw *The Night Watch* by Rembrandt, several marvelous paintings by Johannes Vermeer, and others by Van Gogh. Taking the tram back to our hotel, the boys quickly zonked out, having watched movies during the flight across the Atlantic. Nonetheless, we felt that the excursion dramatically opened their eyes to another culture—one where the people looked like us but spoke and lived differently.

The next morning, we boarded our flight to Arusha, Tanzania. I had read from the U.S. State Department advisories warning tourists of potential trouble in Arusha, but we were safe within a guarded compound. We met our guides and discussed the next few days' journey. Soon after, we took a jeep to the Serengeti and started seeing a few animals and birds. At one point, our grandson Daniel wandered off but was quickly found talking with another group of tourists. We later traveled to the tented camp where we would stay for several days. There we were joined by a couple from Ecuador. The husband was a tour guide in the same company for tourists in Ecuador while the wife was a teacher. They took an immediate liking to our three grandsons.

From the camp, we set out on expeditions and saw a variety of animals: water buffaloes, lions, hyenas, elephants, and hippos. The boys subsisted on spaghetti, which our cook expertly prepared. At night, after dinner, we made our way back to our tents. It was eerie, with the luminous eyes of animals following in the dark. Occasionally we heard lions growling, but nothing happened. The next day we ventured out again, this time spotting giraffes and leopards from our jeep.

A few tsetse flies hovering around prompted our youngest grandson, Conner, to shield himself in a sweatshirt pulled up above his nose, a gimme hat, and aviator sunglasses. At night, the Ecuadorian couple played cards with the boys. Moving on, we traveled to a small airfield where bush pilots flew groups of tourists in and out of the airstrip. Our oldest grandson, Spencer, had always been fascinated by flight, and he was mesmerized by what he saw. Earlier, while we waited to depart Houston, he had looked out the lounge window and watched the aircraft land and take off with great interest.

A few years after our trip, Spencer graduated from college with a business degree but decided against that path. Instead, he took flight lessons. Today, he is an airline pilot. Travel can not only broaden your interests—it can change your life.

We later visited an elementary school in the bush, where the children smiled warmly despite their tattered clothing. Our boys later joined them to play basketball. The children had doubtless not seen many white families with kids their age, and the experience was eye-opening for all of them. We were highly satisfied that our boys' horizons had been profoundly widened.

Not long after, we convinced our daughter-in-law that we could safely take her and Barry's sons, Jimmy, Johnny, and Robby to Costa Rica. It was Easter, and San Jose was empty. We met our guide and set out to see natural sights, including a large waterfall, a butterfly center, and a rainforest. We stopped at a farm (without later informing U.S. Customs) where the boys milked cows. "So this is where milk comes from!" one of them exclaimed. Later, we went zip-lining, an adventure I was certain would send me plummeting to my death six hundred feet below. We also visited a small resort with a swimming pool, a patio, and an iguana named Whiskey.

Later, as part of our fiftieth anniversary celebration, we decided to take our two sons and their six sons to Italy. The trip was hugely expensive, but we wanted to make a lasting impact on our boys' worldviews. We also brought our daughter-in-law and Betty's sister, rounding out a full travel group. The twelve of us met in Amsterdam and flew to Florence. From there, we immediately boarded a bus to Lucca, Puccini's hometown. We thoroughly enjoyed the city—the food, the music, and a side trip to Pisa. In Pisa, which Betty and I had visited in 1966 when there were far fewer tourists, we climbed the tower again, although with more difficulty this time. It seemed the tower was leaning at a sharper angle.

Back in Lucca, we dined at a variety of restaurants. At one outdoor restaurant, one of the boys, Robby, ordered shrimp scampi. When he requested for parmesan cheese on top, the response was immediate: "No! No! *Non puoi. Non mettere il formaggio sui gamberi*! *Devi essere impazzito*!"—in English, "No! No! You cannot. Don't put cheese on shrimp! You must be out of your mind!" It seemed a little harsh when yelled at an eight-year-old American kid, but the point was clear. Fortunately, Robby is not easily intimidated and cares little about boundaries. Later, we passed a bronze statue of Puccini with his legs crossed. As I photographed the statue surrounded by our family, I noticed Robby reclining in Puccini's bronze lap.

In 2014, Betty and I joined a small group of friends on a journey to Cuba. In Havana, we exchanged our U.S. currency for CUCs, the regime's way to directly sequester hard currency. We visited the *Club Floridita,* where we stood beside Hemmingway's statue, and enjoyed one of his famous daiquiris. We rode in perfectly restored ancient American cars from the 1950s, toured the waterfront esplanade, the Malecon, tried our Cuban Spanish against our Mexican Spanish, visited art museums, drank *mojitos,* watched brilliant dance troupes, and traveled to towns in the interior. It was all fascinating.

Fidel was ill, Raul Castro was president, and the economy was a basket case, which Cubans attributed to the American blockade. Regardless, Cuba was said to have good health care, although we picked up a hitchhiker—a young doctor from Columbia—who was destitute. I bought some artwork by locals, which pleased us both. We also visited an old folks' home, and there was an elderly lady who was hard of hearing. I had an old pair of hearing aids and a few batteries and gave them to her. Her face lit up, and my heart soared.

Also in 2014, we traveled to the former Yugoslavia. Our trip began in Dubrovnik, a destination that had been on my checklist for more than forty years, ever since a senior partner at the firm where I worked visited on a business development junket. It is a delightful city on the coast of the Adriatic, as is Croatia, in which it belongs. This region was once part of Yugoslavia, a state ruled by Generalissimo Tito, whose origins were a combination of several Slavic states, which was an important factor in unifying its diverse sub-states. Although his rule was Communist, it remained stubbornly independent from Moscow.

We also went to Zagreb, whose old town situates above the modern city. Zagreb offered fascinating sites, including Zrinjevac Park and the Museum of Broken Relationships, which explores sadness and loss resulting from the aftermath of breaking up with someone you love or once loved. We also discovered the Croatian Museum of Naïve Art, with a fine display of outsider artworks.

Later, we visited Montenegro and the Bay of Kotar, a beautiful harbor stuffed with the luxury cabin cruisers—floating palaces of Russian plutocrats and oligarchs. We also visited Mostar in Bosnia-Herzegovina, with its graceful bridge, and Sarajevo, the site of many battles between the Bosnian Serb army and the residents of other faiths. The holes in buildings and sidewalks reminded me of a book I had read, *The Cellist of Sarajevo*, about a member of the symphony who braved snipers' billets and mortars to play his cello, sitting in his stool in a tuxedo during wartime, with sniper fire surrounding him, offering a plea for peace and sanity for twenty-two days during what came to be called The Breadline Massacre.

In Slovenia, the home country of Melania Trump, there was a crude wooden statue of her commissioned by an American artist. When the sculpture was chopped down for a July 4 bonfire, it was replaced by a bronze version. We missed seeing both. In Ljubljana, we visited their provocative contemporary art museum before heading home.

With a group of six friends, we traveled to Morocco. After landing in Constantinople, we took a bus trip north to Chefchaouen, nicknamed "The Blue City" because so many of its buildings are washed in blue pigment. It is a quant, picturesque town filled with shops and cafés. Founded in the 1400s by Moorish exiles from Spain, Chefchaouen's strategic location made it a destination for caravans traveling from the Rif Mountains and the Mediterranean into the interior of Morocco. The blue walls, it is said, help keep mosquitos away.

Later we traveled to Rabat and then to Fes. Afterward, we made our way across the Atlas Mountains, spending two nights in the sweltering desert, sleeping in tents. We rode camels in a long procession, one after another. I had the impression that the camel behind me was beginning to fall in love, occasionally nudging me with its nose and even resting its head on my lap. Afterward we visited a date farmer who showed us that he was a dowser, demonstrating his gift by finding water with his forked branch. Along the way, we discovered that we could shop for groceries. In this Muslim country, alcohol was officially frowned upon, but groceries sold wine out the back door, tucked into paper bags.

Later, when we reached Marrakesh, we found a huge liquor store that was not advertised as such but which was well-known to the locals. It was crowded with men, and for all the world looked like any liquor store in the States. I made the mistake of taking a photograph and was immediately threatened by two men who evidently didn't want any evidence of their presence there. They leaned over me menacingly while I showed them that I removed the photos.

We also visited the central square in Marrakesh, where several snake charmers coaxed their cobras. A skit was performed by two street entertainers: one with a headband with rubber sandals inserted on each side to resemble donkey ears while the other berated him loudly in Arabic.

When we returned to Casablanca to catch our flight out, we noticed a place with a sign indicating it was "Rick's Bar of Casablanca." On our way back through Paris, we took the others to our favorite bistro, Chez Rene', on Boulevard Saint-Germain. We enjoyed a wonderful beef bourguignon, served by a delightful waiter named Daniel. We stayed in an inexpensive hotel nearby in the 5th, which has since become *tres cher*.

Later, we traveled to Scandinavia, beginning in Oslo. We booked passage on the Hurtigruten packet line to sail along Norway's west coast, from Bergen to Kirkines, above the Arctic Circle and near Murmansk in Russia. Along the way, we visited the Lofoten War Memorial Museum in Svolvær, which exhibits curiosities and rare items from everyday life during the war, including Nazi uniforms, cigarette packages, condoms, and even Christmas decorations adorned with swastikas. Among its display is a painting that may have been created by Adolf Hitler, containing four sketches of Disney cartoon characters signed "A. H."

We also went to northern Finland, through what we mistakenly call *Lapland*, inhabited largely by the Saami people. These people have massive herds of reindeer, often several thousand in number, and somehow can distinguish members of their own herd from others.

We saw a pervasive presence of electric vehicles, mostly Teslas, and charging stations. As is true in much of Scandinavia, taxes are very high, but medical care is first-rate and free, as is education. Although they are members of NATO and provide for their own defense, they do not bear the enormous expense of maintaining a massive, globally dispersed military, as we do.

From there we returned to Italy, beginning in Naples. We visited Pompeii more thoroughly this time, traveled to Sorrento, Positano, Salerno, and Paestum, with its fine ruined temples and museum. Next, we left for Sicily, where we visited Catania, hiked on Mount Etna, which fortunately was dormant, and ended in Syracuse, where the old town, Ortygia, is full of visual wonders. In Malta, we primarily stayed in Valletta, although we also visited **Ħaġar Qim,** a megalithic temple complex dating back to around 3600–3200 BC. It features large stone blocks and intricate carvings.

Back in Valletta, we sought out St. John's Cathedral to see Caravaggio's *Beheading of St. John the Baptist.* In 1607, the brilliant but dissolute Italian master painter was fleeing from justice in Rome for killing a man. By 1608, he was in serious trouble again and made a breathtaking escape, fleeing Malta by boat to Sicily.

In 2018, we signed up for a trip to Bavaria, starting on our own in Berlin. I had previously been to the city in 1994 doing some consulting work on the Sony Center on Potsdamer Platz, home of the world's first traffic signal. Back then, I went for morning runs in the Tiergarten, also known as "animal park," of 520-acre expanse west of Sony Center. This time I had a chance to do more sightseeing. We went to *KaDeWe*, or KDW, a vast six-story luxury department store, where we bought coffee on the sixth floor and then wandered through its interesting and artful displays. We saw sections of the wall still standing, covered with street art and graffiti. We also visited the Brandenburg Gate, with its six columns and four horses, the former scene of JFK's *Icb bin ein Berliner* (I am a Berliner) speech. Just beyond stood the restored Reichstag Building (Parliament), topped by a glass dome designed by Britain's Norman Foster, and a ramp circling upward. The Holocaust Memorial, by American architect, Peter Eisenman, is a bewildering display of ranks of 2,711 concrete pillars ranging in size from zero to four meters, and reminiscent of some Jewish graveyards. It is possible to lose oneself among these positive and negative spaces, overwhelmed by their sheer number and individuality.

Taking a train from Berlin, we arrived in Prague. The contrast between modern Prague and 1990 was startling. No more little guys with open suitcases selling cheap crystal, no more empty store window displays. The Communist and the post-Communist eras had faded away. In their place was a thoroughly modern public citizenry, comfortable with edgy literature and art. Echoes of the past remained, but they were overwhelmed by an urgent present. There was still the timeless procession of apostles at the restored clock tower, and surprises around almost every corner. However, it was clear that the Czech Republic had entered the twenty-first century.

In 2018, we made a second trip—my third—to Turkey, where we first stayed in Istanbul. There we visited the labyrinthine Grand Bazaar, the Hagia Sophia, and the Blue Mosque, and strolled the streets. We came across an alterations shop that advertised itself as a "Taylor" shop and an ATM machine with a sign that read, "Don't Working." I shudder to think how badly we might mangle Turkish if we attempted to use it on our signage back home. From Istanbul we traveled to Konya, and then to Cappadocia, where we saw the volcanic remains of rock chimneys and flew above them in a hot-air balloon. One of the most amazing parts of the balloon trip was the landing—not on stable ground, but on a speeding flatbed truck. We returned to Istanbul through Anatalya and Izmir.

Earlier, while working in Saudi Arabia, I made a mid-flight stop in Izmir in an attempt to meet up with John, one of the two dropouts who had inspired me to travel. He was working for the U.S. Air Force, teaching history at a local high school. This was my second attempt to find him. The first time I flew from Dhahran to Istanbul and caught a cigarette smoke-filled Turkish Airlines flight to Izmir but after landing had no idea how to locate him. I tried the police, but we had no common language to discuss the matter. On this second attempt, I followed some people who spoke English. When I asked about the American school, they knew exactly where it was; in fact, they knew where my friend lived.

Note to self: *It's a big world. Try to get more information about your destinations before leaving.*

EPILOGUE

What have I learned?

The huge advantage of DIY travel is that there is no way you can predict what may happen that you can learn from, or the value of those insights. There is no better way to understand a place than by interacting with its people. Travel stimulates our minds and keeps us off-balance just enough that we are forced to adapt and learn.

While guided tours are useful in terms of assurances of safety, avoiding disappointing or faulty arrangements, they may also prevent you from having spontaneous and unexpected experiences that can be enlightening and invaluable.

We all have many things in common. While no single culture knows everything of value, we can all learn from others. Assumptions about another culture can be faulty. I'm reminded of one fellow traveler as we went through India who exclaimed, "These people don't have enough self-respect to keep their homes [hovels] in order." True story.

Some quotations about travel:

"Where do people and nations go to find new things to believe in, new values to orient their lives around? Where do they go to revive their humanistic core? They find these things in the realm of culture" (David Brooks).

"Tourists don't know where they've been, travelers don't know where they're going. Travel is glamorous only in retrospect" (Paul Theroux).

"There are two worlds: the world of the tourist and the world of everyone else" (Anthony Bourdain).

"Just look at those people, running around with so little clothing on. They can't even speak Spanish properly; nobody can understand what they're saying. Sure, they're smiling and laughing a lot but it's just because they don't realize what a miserable life they're living. Well, we'll fix that: Get them into church and teach them how sinful they are and how ashamed they should be. I know it's hot, but wrap them up in animal skins to cover themselves and avoid shame and embarrassment. Make them more resistant to disease by exposing them a bit to some of the guys in the brig" (C. Columbus).

9 798890 521150